MATHEMATICS
MADE MEANINGFUL

by JOHN KUNZ

A Guidebook for teachers, parents, and others who wish to help children in their study of mathematics. For correlated use with the world-famous Cuisenaire® colored rods and the step-by-step Activity Cards.

CUISENAIRE COMPANY OF AMERICA, INC.

Printed in U.S.A.
ISBN 0-914040-03-0

1 2 3 4 5 6 7 8 9 10 BK 97969594

Cuisenaire Company of America, Inc.
10 Bank St., P.O. Box 5026
White Plains, N.Y. 10602-5026

TABLE OF CONTENTS

TITLES OF ACTIVITY CARDS

INTRODUCTION

Series A:

A-1	First Games
A-2	Staircases
A-3A	Train Games
A-3B	Sequences
A-4	Matching
A-5A	Triplets
A-5B	Symmetry
A-6	Using Number Names

Series B:

B-1	Equations
B-2A	Variables
B-2B	Inequalities
B-3	Patterns
B-4	Numerals

Series C:

C-1	Introduction (to Sets)
C-2A	Sets
C-2B	Subsets
C-3	Equal & Equivalent Sets
C-4	Union & Intersection

Series D:

D-1	Introduction (to Arithmetic)
D-2	Measuring
D-3	Unit Fractions
D-4	Non-Unit Fractions
D-5	Comparing Rods

Series E:

E-1	Introduction (to Numbers)
E-2	Patterns of Numbers
E-3A	Complements
E-3B	Parentheses
E-4	Prime & Composite Numbers
E-5	Numbers to One-Hundred

Series F:

F-1	Reading Large Numbers
F-2A	Trains Longer than Orange
F-2B	Choosing Problems
F-3	Finding Products
F-4	Factors & Multiples

Series G:

G-1	Equivalent Expressions
G-2	Hints for Addition
G-3	Hints for Subtraction
G-4	Hints for Multiplication
G-5	Hints for Division

Series H:

H-1	Fractions & Reciprocals
H-2	Equivalent Fractions
H-3	Adding Fractions
H-4	Multiplying Fractions
H-5	Dividing Fractions

Series I:

I-1	Towers & Place Value
I-2	Powers
I-3	Coefficients & Exponents
I-4	Non-Decimal Bases
I-5	Carrying & Place Value

Series J:

J-1	Negative Numbers
J-2	Negative Numbers
J-3	Multiplying Signed Numbers

Series K:

K-1	Metric Length
K-2A	Metric Area
K-2B	Metric Area
K-3	Metric Volume, Capacity, & Mass

I

PREFACE

PREFACE

This Guidebook is designed for those who wish to help children in their study of mathematics. It is an integral part of two Cuisenaire study kits. the *"Mathematics Made Meaningful"* Kit (school edition), and the *"Cuisenaire Home Mathematics Kit"* (home edition). It is for correlated use with the world-famous Cuisenaire® colored rods (with which any child can promptly see and prove basic number relationships), and the step-by-step Activity Cards, supplied with each Kit.

(This Kit emphasizes the arithmetic and number areas of mathematics. For the study of geometry, the Cuisenaire Geoboard is a recommended model. It is a square plastic board with pegs on two faces. one a square lattice, the other a circular lattice. By stretching rubber bands around the carefully-positioned pegs, the child can learn much about geometric relationships. The Cuisenaire Geoboard is available from the publisher of this Kit. A section of this Guidebook is devoted to the use of the electronic hand-calculator (page 53), but there are no Activity Cards on this topic; several excellent books on calculators are listed in the Bibliography (page 87).)

It is not necessary to read this Guidebook in order to use the Activity Cards and the Cuisenaire rods with your child. The Activity Cards are sequential; a child may be able to go through them without guidance from this book. Many topics are not treated here because they are covered in detail in the Activity Cards. For this reason. it is important that when you find a cross-reference in this Guidebook or its Glossary (section VI) to the Activity Cards. you should read the appropriate Card. Similarly, you will find references in the Glossary both to this book and to the Activity Cards, as they are designed to complement each other.

Much of the material covered in the Activity Cards is purposely explained for the adult in this Guidebook, not in the Activity Cards. It should enable you to help your child more effectively, as well as help you understand what is happening in mathematics education. It may also increase your own understanding of and interest in mathematics!

(Reference throughout this Guidebook to *"your child"* may be interpreted appropriately by parent, teacher, or other adult, as any child using this kit for help in the study of mathematics.)

You are probably well aware of the revolutionary changes taking place in mathematics programs, from kindergarten through high school. Educators are awake to the fact that our world of today rests on science . . . and science rests on mathematics. Science, business and industry increasingly demand men and women who can describe scientific findings accurately, who are able to understand, program, and interpret the output of our computers and automated machines, and who can deal with the mathematics required to cope with advanced science, technology, and other complex new fields of knowledge. So, a complete understanding of fundamental mathematical concepts is vitally important for your child.

The terms 'modern math' and 'new math' are somewhat misleading. Actually, mathematics has expanded at least as much as physics, chemistry, or biology over the years to keep pace with scientific accomplishment. The changes implied by the term 'new math' include not only the changes in subject matter, however, but also changes in the approach to teaching mathematics.

Fundamental to today's mathematics is the emphasis on the 'discovery' method of teaching, a far cry from the memorization of facts and teaching-by-rote which children have endured in the past. Now the child discovers the basic principles himself. He still develops skills in computation but they are placed in a different context and the reasons behind them are made crystal clear.

One of the most valuable tools for children to use in discovering mathematics are the Cuisenaire colored rods. In country after country around the world these materials have made it possible for children to explore the study of patterns and relationships which we call mathematics, and have enabled children to discover their own creative abilities.

WHY THIS STUDY KIT?

It is not always possible for a child to have personal instruction from his teacher when misunderstandings in mathematics develop. Crowded classrooms, illness, substitute teachers, lack of attention, unscheduled interruptions or abbreviations of a program because of bad weather or school functions—any one of these or other reasons can handicap your child in securing a thorough understanding of basic mathematical concepts.

Many adults are stumped when children seek extra help in math. The Cuisenaire Mathematics Study Kit has been designed to help answer this problem. For the first time, the world-famous Cuisenaire rods are available for use in an integrated package planned as a supplementary aid in math—for child *and* adult!

(The Cuisenaire approach to mathematical understanding has been rigorously tested for many years in classroom use. With Cuisenaire rods, children can promptly see and prove basic number relationships. The rods are endorsed by leading educators and are used daily by schools in all 50 states of the U.S. and throughout the world.)

Mathematics, as presented by the Cuisenaire Mathematics Study Kit, is easy for your child to grasp and understand. It will also be easy for you, the adult, *if you treat it as a new subject—a new game to enjoy! Do not attempt to solve all the problems introduced in this Kit by using the 'old math' you learned in elementary school.* The Kit deliberately follows the present-day pattern of integrating algebra and arithmetic. *Its use will not conflict in any way with the specific mathematics program your child learns in school.* Instead, it will help him to understand and make better progress in his program.

Your child may or may not already be using Cuisenaire colored rods in school. This Kit may be used in either case, without any hesitation. Like the world globe and map used with different geography textbooks, this Kit may be used as enrichment for any school mathematics program.

Although the Cuisenaire rods are usually used in the average

11

classroom with its normal range of abilities, they have proved to be of great value in many special learning areas.

USE WITH EXCEPTIONAL CHILDREN

BLIND CHILDREN

Blind children handle the rods with great facility. The development of their tactile sense is such that they can easily distinguish the different lengths—which, just like sighted children, they call by their color names. With the rods it has been demonstrated that sightless children who are otherwise normal need not be handicapped insofar as mathematical skills are concerned. In fact, the rods offer blind children a rich and powerful vehicle by which they can enter into the world of mathematics without experiencing the need for written notation. They become capable of sustained, accurate, and rapid mental calculation through the establishment of a multitude of number relations.

DEAF CHILDREN

Because so many mathematical relationships can be seen directly with the rods, much of the dependence on verbalization for understanding these relationships can be avoided. The notation can be immediately related to the observed structures.

MENTALLY RETARDED CHILDREN

These children particularly need to develop a sense of confidence in their ability to solve a problem themselves, and to be certain their answer is right. The rods enable the retarded child to do this. He can use the rods to find the solution to a problem, and from what he sees be *sure* he is right. The criterion for knowing he is right is not whether the teacher smiles—a poor criterion, for it does not help him to know *why* the answer was right. Again, when the answer has been found first without rods, the child can check with the rods and *know* whether he was right, and, if not, correct his own answer. This is true for all children, but is particularly important for the retarded.

GIFTED CHILDREN

Because the rods are a model for the set of rational numbers, they can be used to suggest many mathematical relationships, and for a bright child this will occur without the teacher necessarily having to intervene. For example, in a class where one or two of the pupils are able to move much more rapidly than the others, it is found that when they have done what is asked of all the class they will on their own start doing more with the rods. This may take the form of going further with the same activity, or of using the opportunity to explore some other relationships that the rods have suggested. In this way the gifted child is helped to avoid the real dangers of boredom in a setting where he can do more than the others.

EMOTIONALLY DISTURBED CHILDREN

Teachers have found the rods very helpful for many children with emotional problems. The rods are attractive and attention-holding. Because the child himself can control the use of the rods, and find the relationships embodied in the rods, it is a situation with no threat to him. He can move in his own way. Often this will facilitate having the child participate more easily in activities with the rest of the class.

CONTENTS OF THE KIT:

- Guidebook: **"Mathematics Made Meaningful"**

- Set of 50 **Activity Cards** grouped in 11 series (each series separated by color and ordered by difficulty) and designed to be used by the adult in working with a child through the basics of mathematics.

- Set of 155 **Cuisenaire Colored Rods** (in a self-sorting plastic tray), one square-centimetre in cross-section, in lengths ranging from 1 centimetre to 10 centimetres, without confining unit measurement marks.

II
CUISENAIRE® COLORED RODS
AND THE
MATHEMATICS CURRICULUM

THE STORY OF THE RODS

For thousands of years man has used various objects as counters in his first exploration of numbers. The Greeks and Romans used small stones or counters, thereby giving us the root of the word *calculate* which stems from the Latin *"calculus"*—a pebble or small stone. Thus, calculating means "pebbling" or reckoning with small stones.

During the past centuries, models and drawings of various kinds have been used to make the meaning of mathematics clearer to students. A really good model can be of powerful help in learning to see relationships. An example familiar to all is the use of globes and maps in learning geography. Imagine how hard it would be to learn geography without maps or globes available! Use of a well-designed globe to study the earth makes it easy to see immediately such relationships as water versus land areas, or where one place is located in relation to another, etc. The more time one spends exploring maps and globes, the more one knows about the world they model.

In the early 1930's, a Belgian school teacher began a series of experiments which eventually resulted in the invention of a remarkable model—the Cuisenaire® colored rods. M. Georges Cuisenaire was born in Thuin, Belgium, in 1891. His educational background included both the study of music and education. After training as a composer in the Conservatory, he became a teacher, then an elementary principal. He retired 35 years later as Director of Education for his school district, and died January 1, 1976.

While an elementary principal, Cuisenaire was anxious to find an easy way for his students to enjoy the learning of arithmetic. As a composer aware of the relationship between mathematics and music, he was convinced that children could enjoy learning mathematics just as much as they enjoyed learning music with him. Through his lifelong knowledge of music, he arrived at the idea of expressing numbers in color. Knowing that the notes in music are based on specific mathematical intervals, Cuisenaire conceived the idea of a colored keyboard that could be used to show related and unrelated combinations of notes. He then amplified this concept to apply to more general mathematical relationships. In 1952, after 20 years of experimenting, he introduced his colored rods.

Cuisenaire's colored rods were such a success with his pupils that their use spread to neighboring areas. Eventually they found their way into classrooms around the world. In June, 1965, the Belgian government honored Cuisenaire with the title "Officer of the Order of Leopold II" for his discovery of the colored rods. His government also gave him many additional honors for his work in education. Cuisenaire's colored rods were chosen for display at the Belgian pavilion at "Hemisfair," the World Fair held in 1968 in San Antonio, Texas.

In country after country, and in every one of the 50 states in the U. S., educators have embraced M. Georges Cuisenaire's "colored sticks" and, in the process, have performed a revolution in the teaching of mathematics. They have seen children master arithmetic with ease and joy, and reverse their attitude toward it from apathy or resistance to enthusiastic participation. Just as a globe is used in many different settings, the colored rods are now used to explore many different mathematical relationships in many different school settings ranging from preschool through college!

The colored sticks that wrought this change are as simple looking as the equation $2+2=4$. The rods, one square centimetre in cross-section, increase by one-centimetre steps from one to ten centimetres in length, and are of different colors according to their lengths. Yet with them can be expressed an almost unlimited range of mathematical relationships.

The colors of the rods serve two purposes — psychological and mathematical — that are fundamental to the entire Cuisenaire idea. The first, and more obvious, is that the appeal to children of bright colors invites their uninhibited play, construction, and manipulation. Through this beginning play, the children make innumerable discoveries about the relationships among rods of the same and different colors.

The second function of color is that it permits identification of the otherwise unmarked rod lengths by their color names rather than by assigned number values. As they perform various operations, the children can discuss their results in terms of immediately perceived color, rather than memorized number names. Once the operations and relationships are understood, number names, mental calculation, and written notation are naturally and easily introduced and substituted.

The coloring of the rods is not haphazard, as may at first appear. The unit rod is white, for it is basic, and inherent in all other lengths. The rods of lengths 2, 4, and 8 centimetres are red, purple, and brown respectively. Those that are 3, 6, and 9 centimetres long are light green, dark green, and blue. The 5 and 10 centimetre lengths are yellow and orange. Black is assigned to the 7 centimetre length, which does not belong to any of the other families.

The adult's role, in the setting provided by the rods, is to observe and to ask questions about what the children are discovering for themselves, rather than to instruct or explain. It is certainly common knowledge that anyone, child or adult, will more readily learn and more permanently retain facts and ideas that he has worked out for himself, as against a series of words that are not made meaningful to him through his own experience.

The power of making abstractions is at its peak in 6-to-9-year-olds. At this age, children's curiosity, their desire to create, and their ability to form new concepts have not yet been dulled. The Cuisenaire rods, which allow free rein to this natural curiosity and creativity, are now in use in many thousands of classrooms around the world. Visitors to these classrooms are usually amazed at the feats of mathematical skill the young pupils perform, perhaps without realizing that children have many remarkable abilities which our education systems are only beginning to understand and exploit.

CUISENAIRE'S PHILOSOPHY OF ACTIVE TEACHING

SEEING:
- Numbers and their multiples are represented by related colors.
- The various lengths, being of regular gradation, permit active use of eyes and hands.
- Dimensions and colors constitute a double link between numbers. This classification facilitates the identification of

numbers, their groupings, and the discovery of the relationships between them; ensures that they are precisely and firmly fixed in the memory; and prepares the way for mental perception.

DOING.

- The child's need for action finds an outlet in the spontaneous construction of numerous combinations, freely produced by him and based only upon his awareness of relationships and groupings of numbers. These combinations permit a great variety of decompositions.

UNDERSTANDING.

- Seeing and doing lead to conviction and to ease in retaining results. The imagination is stimulated and reckoning becomes automatic.

RECKONING

- Through manipulating the rods, the child discovers new combinations which increase not only his skill in calculating, but also his interest, experience, and knowledge.

VERIFICATION.

- This is an important phase of the child's experimental work, for he checks his own results and learns to rely on his own criteria for correcting his mistakes.

Thus, by the use of this method of colored numbers.

- Each child starts from the beginning and is compelled to rediscover arithmetic for himself, at his own pace and according to his own capacity.
- Visual, muscular and tactile images, clearly defined and durable, are created.
- Each number acquires and retains its individuality in the numerous combinations and decompositions in which it and its various multiples play a part.
- The child is gradually brought to a certain level of abstraction through repeated practice in seeing mentally.
- Since it is the child's *own* thought which takes material form through *his own* manipulations and with the active intervention of all *his* senses (colors and dimensions thus being constructively associated), his analytic capacity is developed

through *his own* calculations and *his own* experience. He acquires, without strain, mental flexibility and an attitude of objectivity.

- Work becomes attractive and interesting, time is saved, and the teacher's task is simplified.
- The bridge is formed between the early experience gained through play and observation, and the stage of systematic work.

WHAT IS TODAY'S MATH LIKE?

The content of school mathematics programs has been changing rapidly. The change involves both a rearrangement of mathematics previously taught in elementary and high school and the introduction of 'new' material not previously part of the mathematics curriculum. Therefore, the term 'modern mathematics' or the 'new math' is used to mean a change in the sequence of material now taught, as well as the addition of specific new content.

Until recently, arithmetic was taught in elementary school and algebra in high school. The artificial distinction between the two, however, is disappearing and a combination of algebra and arithmetic is being taught in school classes from kindergarten through secondary school. Algebra makes it possible for the child to understand the essential structure of a mathematical system. He then understands much better what he learns about numbers in arithmetic.

More than a dozen mathematics programs, each with slight variations around a basic norm, have been evolved by educators and publishers in recent years. All programs, while differing in detail, stress the "structure" of mathematics—the way number systems are built up and the laws that govern their behavior. Different schools may follow slightly different sequences of study but, essentially, your child's school mathematics program encourages him to learn the 'why' of mathematics, to understand more fully why the number manipulations he performs are valid. He finds out *for himself* about the world of numbers, and an intellectually intriguing study becomes fun as he learns better and faster.

MATHEMATICS IN THE ELEMENTARY SCHOOL

Much emphasis is placed these days on 'modern math.' This phrase, as used by different people, has several meanings. To the mathematician it has by custom meant certain topics in mathematics, which by historical accident became known as modern mathematics. The phrase and topics were established by the turn of the century, and do not in this sense imply the mathematics currently being discovered and explored by mathematicians.

Some of these turn-of-the-century topics, including in particular the simplest elements of the theory of sets, in recent years have found their way into the elementary and secondary curricula. In this sense 'modern math' is often taken to mean any way of teaching which brings in some of the language of sets. However, the actual amount of set theory covered is usually very slight in comparison with the degree to which the theory is developed in mathematics. Mathematicians themselves are split as to the importance of set theory as a foundation for mathematics.

Another use of the term "modern math" is the stress on "meaning" in learning mathematics—that is, an understanding of basic principles and their application in distinction to the rote memorization of procedures which was so long encouraged. In the elementary school, this has meant inclusion of some of the simple algebraic properties—the commutative, associative, and distributive axioms, for example—underlying arithmetic.

Yet another, and looser, meaning is sometimes given to "modern math," to indicate that some new attention is to be given to the teaching of arithmetic, to bring it "up to date." In this sense, the phrase has become a catch-all for the new concern with mathematics education which has prevailed in the United States since Sputnik.

In essence, the different meanings attached to "modern mathematics" agree in the emphasis on the structure of mathematics, and on the student's gaining a greater ability in mathematics through understanding this structure and its applications. In the December, 1964 issue of the *The Arithmetic Teacher,* Dr. Donald Inbody summarized it in this way:

"Traditional mathematics instruction has been concerned with 'how,' and has done a pretty good job of that. The newer programs are concerned with 'why' *and* 'how.' There is really no great mystery involved. The newer emphasis is different, but the difference has bothered adults more than it has children. More and more children are coming to find mathematics interesting and exciting. Teachers and parents are making the same discovery."

The Cuisenaire rods are used successfully both in programs which emphasize the use of sets as an introduction to mathematics as well as in programs which stress other algebraic properties first and bring in a fuller treatment of set theory later. The Cuisenaire Company of America publishes a number of books on the use of the rods. These include usage from kindergarten through high school.

It is therefore possible to use the Cuisenaire rods as a model with most of the programs in modern mathematics which have been developed. Just as a map can be used with many geography texts, so the rods are compatible with any good mathematics program. However, the programs built specifically around the use of the rods make possible much more effective exploitation of the mathematics embodied in the rods. The Cuisenaire rods and books are designed together to enable children to discover, master, and enjoy the principles of mathematics. Schools using the Cuisenaire system exclusively have achieved remarkable success.

WHAT DOES YOUR CHILD LEARN IN MATHEMATICS?

Mathematics is a study of quantities and relationships which uses the language of numbers and symbols. As your child advances in this useful field of human knowledge, from early childhood through college, he will follow certain learning patterns involving language, notation, operations, and relationships.

He will learn a new language in mathematics. New words will

enter his vocabulary. Old words, used in everyday language, will take on special meaning in mathematics. Some of this language is written with numerals and special symbols which we call *mathematical notation*. These symbols are *not* mathematical ideas but merely a way of writing names for such ideas. Notation makes it easy to describe the relationships of mathematics and easier to perform long computations.

Your child will use notation to investigate and understand mathematical relationships between various numbers and objects. These relationships fit together to form a mathematical structure which he can use to solve particular problems. The more he knows about these relationships, the easier it will be for him to visualize the structure of a new mathematical situation, predict what will happen in a specific mathematical operation, and know how to arrive at a solution.

Your child will learn to perform certain operations on mathematical elements, such as addition, subtraction, multiplication, division, square root, union, intersection, complement, and others. He will discover the relationship between these operations and then see the overall structure of mathematics and the general principles, laws, or axioms governing these operations.

Some mathematical language must be memorized, such as the series of names we use in counting (one, two, three, etc.). Other words have been chosen so that their everyday meaning helps us to use and understand them in their mathematical meaning. Consider the word *set*. A *set* of chinaware, for example, helps one understand that a *set* is a well-defined collection of objects . . . or of ideas, numbers, persons or things. Even though the use of sets in mathematics may seem strange, the language about sets is easy to learn because it is closely related to our everyday use and understanding of such words. Precise use of words is important in mathematics; but most important is understanding the ideas which they represent.

Only a small part of your child's important growth in mathematical understanding will come through memorizing a series of separate facts. The new mathematical language, its special notation and memorized facts—all will keep returning in new ways to reinforce your child's memory as he learns more mathematics. Most important will be his developing understanding of mathematical structure, the operations and relationships that comprise it. Once this structure is clearly apparent to him, he can easily discover and develop new relationships which can be built on the ones he already knows.

The mathematics programs now in use throughout the United States place great stress on the importance of understanding the structure and meaning behind mathematical operations, and less emphasis on the simple memorization of the specific techniques of those operations and their use in solving problems. This stress on meaning, incidentally, makes today's child better at mathematical computation than children were in the past, even though the methods he uses may seem strange or even slow to some adults. Computational skills in arithmetic will not be sufficient for your child as an adult in the future. Much of routine computation will be handled by automated machines. An understanding of mathematical structure and relationships, however, will be vitally important. Extra time and effort spent in the beginning to develop your child's understanding of meaning will pay off in increased knowledge later.

Your child will learn some language in mathematics which will be familiar to you; some will seem strange. Many of the mathematical ideas expressed are identical with those you had in school but others are not. All of it—language and ideas—is new to your child. That which is new to you he will learn as easily as the mathematical language and ideas you once learned in school. However, emphasis on understanding, coupled with accurate use of mathematical language, makes it easier for him to learn mathematics and to express himself more clearly.

III

BASIC RULES OF MATHEMATICS

TWO APPROACHES TO THE UNDERSTANDING OF NUMBER

Mathematics for school children involves several different areas of study. A typical program includes arithmetic, algebra, measurement, geometry, graphing, and probability and statistics. Each day sees new material in other mathematical areas being added to the high school curriculum.

This Kit emphasizes the arithmetic and algebraic areas of mathematics, while referring to some of the things that can be done in other areas such as measurement and geometry. A section at the end of the Activity Cards series, for example, deals with the metric system of measurement, which will be in increasing use in the U.S. in the immediate future.

There are two ways of approaching the idea of 'number' and of working with numbers. The mathematician might describe them as (1) *'discrete'*, meaning separate or distinct, and (2) *'continuous'*, meaning flowing without a break. The school child will find it easier to think of the two approaches in terms of *'counting'*, the naming of separate numerals or things in order, and *'measuring'*, the comparing of a continuous quantity to some standard unit. Counting is a way of answering the question "How many?" Measuring answers the question "How much?"

Both these approaches to number are used and needed in mathematics, and in the work done in schools. The Cuisenaire rods are an excellent model for both approaches and will be used in this Kit to reinforce the understanding of fundamental concepts in mathematics.

The approach to number through counting develops from the idea of the *'set'*, an easy topic to study and understand. The properties of sets are used in the very beginning of mathematics, as well as in its higher realms. This chapter develops some of the fundamentals of sets (which will be very useful in different areas of mathematics), and some of the fundamental notions of operations and the algebraic laws underlying arithmetic.

28

NUMBERS, NUMERALS, AND NOTATION

More attention is being paid in today's mathematics programs to the careful use of language about *numbers* and the *names* for numbers. One of the most important things to understand is that there are many different names for the same number.

The *idea* of the number 'five' is the same, behind all languages, whether you write 'five', 'funf', 'cinq', 'pyat', 'viisi', '5', 'V', or some other meaningful number word. Mathematics is international, although its words and language may change from country to country.

There is a difference between a *number* and a *numeral*. A *number* is an abstract idea which cannot be put on paper. The number 'five', for example, is only the abstract idea for the common property held by all collections of objects which you can match, one for one, with the fingers of one hand. One of the properties shared by all sets {husband, wife}, {father, son}, {apple, pear}, {apple, elephant} is considered as a number. In English, we would call that property 'two' and write it as '2', but there are many other names for this number. All these names for numbers are called numerals.

A *numeral* is a spoken name or a written symbol for a number. You cannot write a number because it is not made of ink or chalk. You cannot write your daughter Jean on paper. You can only write the symbol for your daughter—her name, 'Jean'. We can write the name for the abstract idea of five, either with a word—'five'—or with a figure—'5'. We cannot write a number but we can write a numeral. So we use the word 'numeral' to describe a spoken name or a written figure (such as '5', '37', '1426', etc.) for a number and we use the word 'number, to describe the idea which the numeral represents.

Many different *numerals* can represent the same *number,* just as you may be known by many different names. John Smith may also be called Jack, Honey, Dad, Father, Uncle, etc. He has several names but he is only one person.

Here is an example to illustrate the difference between number and numeral: we know that the number eight is larger than the number five. But which numeral is larger, 5 or 8? Obviously the '5' is larger, in size of type, but the number eight is always larger than the number five.

Here are different names or numerals for the number four:

$$4 \quad 2 + 2 \quad 2^2 \quad 6 - 2 \quad 64 \div 16 \quad 11_3 \quad 18_{\text{mod } 7} \quad 1 \times 4$$

There are many others. Your child will learn some of the many names but he will also learn to distinguish between number and numeral.

The different names for numbers involve ideas of *operation*, *place value*, and *base*.

You are already familiar with the various *operations* which relate numbers together. Addition and multiplication are the two principle operations in arithmetic; subtraction and division are derived from these operations.

There are ten digits (0, 1, 2, 3, 4, 5, 6, 7, 8, 9) in the counting system we use today. They are used in various combinations to write the names of numbers larger than nine. When we write the number 234, this is a short way of writing the following idea.

$$(2 \times 10 \times 10) + (3 \times 10) + (4 \times 1) = 234$$
$$200 \quad + \quad 30 \quad + \quad 4 \quad = 234$$

Each of the digits 2, 3 and 4, used to express 234, has a specific value depending on its place or position in the numeral. In the numeration system we use, if a digit is moved one place to the left, its *place value* increases to ten times that which it had in the place to the right. We call this place value system *base ten*.

Your child probably will learn much about the idea of base in the mathematics taught today. It may be helpful for you to know what this concept means, as it is used in many school math programs.

Our *place value* system is built on the powers of the number ten. It is possible, using the same mathematical principles as are used in base ten, to write the names of numbers using numerals built on the powers of numbers other than ten. For example, there are other numeration systems such as base two, base five, base seven, base twelve, base sixteen, etc. These *non-decimal* numeration systems are often studied in mathematics classes in elementary and junior high school.

What is the meaning of *base* in a numeration system and of what use is it? If you have ever studied algebra, you probably will be able to understand easily the following paragraph. If you have not studied algebra, it will be easier for you to study Activity Card Series I where you will learn about bases.

Our place-value numeration systems use a polynomial (see Glossary) like this to name numbers:

$$ax^3 + bx^2 + cx^1 + dx^0$$

In everyday usage, we assume that x = ten. When we write 2,345, we mean x = 10, a = 2, b = 3, c = 4, and d = 5 in the equation above. Or:

$$2 \times (10)^3 + 3 \times (10)^2 + 4 \times (10)^1 + 5(10)^0 =$$
$$2 \times (10 \times 10 \times 10) + 3 \times (10 \times 10) + 4(10) + 5(1) =$$
$$2000 \quad + \quad 300 \quad + \quad 40 \quad + \quad 5 \quad = \quad 2,345$$

In using other bases we follow the same principles but with the assumption that the x in the equation above represents a number *other than ten*, and with the restriction that the coefficients a, b, c, d etc. must always be smaller than the number used as the base.

Thus, if we were using base five, (to avoid confusion when using a base other than ten, put the name of the base at the end of the numeral) the numeral 234_5 would mean:

$$(2 \times 5 \times 5) + (3 \times 5) + (4 \times 1)$$

or 69 in base ten notation. The study of other bases of notation will definitely help your child understand better the idea of place value.

31

In the past, arithmetic learning consisted largely of many rules for using notation and the special positions in which to place or put each numeral on paper in order to solve arithmetic problems. The emphasis now is on understanding the mathematical meaning behind the procedures; thus, the particular way in which the problem is written is not so important. Your child may change the problem sometimes to another easier form by using a different notation which will still give the same correct answer. He can do this because notation is something he has learned to master.

THE MATHEMATICAL SENTENCE

You already know what a sentence is in the English language. A sentence contains words and conveys a complete thought, and must follow certain rules. We also use the term *mathematical sentence*. In mathematics, a *closed sentence* is a statement which can be determined to be either true or false. Examples are: $5 + 2 = 9$ and $3 \times 4 = 12$. An open sentence is a statement containing a *variable* (such as $\square$ or x or ? etc.), so the truth or falsity of the statement cannot be determined without knowing the value to be assigned to the variable.

Just as an English sentence has nouns, verbs, punctuation, and rules of word order, mathematical sentences have corresponding structure.

The symbols in mathematical sentences serve the same purposes as the words in English sentences. Parentheses ( ) are the most important punctuation marks in mathematical sentences. They indicate that the expression within the parentheses should be considered as a quantity or term in the sentence. An example is in the sentence $5 - (2 + 2) = 1$ where the parentheses indicate that $2 + 2$ is a quantity to be subtracted from 5.

OPERATIONS

We will now re-examine each of the fundamental operations of arithmetic — addition, subtraction, multiplication, and division — and bring together the basic laws for each. We will use the Cuisenaire rods as a tool for insuring a clear understanding of number properties and laws and the essential operations. Where the rods are used for examples in this section, the smallest rod (the white one) is considered to be the unit.

ADDITION (AND SUBTRACTION)

Addition and subtraction are two ways of looking at the same relationship, as will be noted shortly. The laws for the addition of whole numbers and fractions are:

CLOSURE. Addition of numbers results in a number. Thus: 5 + 3 = 8. The numbers added are whole numbers. The answer is a whole number. Using the Cuisenaire Rods, we can show this.

5	3
8	

Similarly, if two fractions are added, the answer will be a fraction. Thus:

$$1/2 + 1/2 = 2/2 \text{ or } 2/4 + 3/4 = 5/4$$

(As shown later on page 74, a whole number can also be expressed as a fraction.)

COMMUTATIVE. The order in which numbers are added does not change the sum.
Thus: 9 + 3 = 3 + 9 = 12

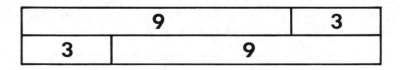

Try this with rods yourself.
Similarly, if a and b represent numbers, then a + b = b + a.

ASSOCIATIVE. Numbers may be grouped in any combination for addition (without changing the order of the terms) without changing the sum. Thus. $(2 + 3) + 4 = 9$ or

$$2 + (3 + 4) = 9 = 5 + 4 = 9 = 2 + 7 = 9.$$

With the Cuisenaire rods, we have.

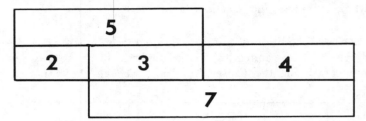

Try this with rods yourself.

IDENTITY ELEMENT. For addition there is a special number, zero (0), which can be added to any number without changing that number. Zero is known as the identity or neutral element for addition. Thus: $5 + 0 = 5$. Or, for any number a, $a + 0 = a$. (With the rods, 0 is no length at all.)

Subtraction is not an independent operation, but is defined in terms of addition. It is called the *inverse operation* to the operation of addition. You can think of subtraction as undoing addition. If you start with 5 and then add 8, you can see that subtracting 8 would undo the effect of adding 8.

$$5 + 8 - 8 = 5 \quad 5 + (8 - 8) = 5 + 0 = 5$$

The rods make it easy to see how the same situation can be described either in terms of addition or of subtraction. Make a 'train' of a yellow rod and a green rod. Place a brown rod side by side with this train as shown below.

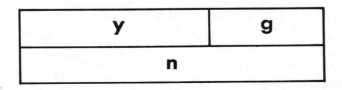

The relationships of the lengths of the above rods can be described equally well as $y + g = n$ or $n - g = y$. Any of these descriptions fit the relationship equally well, and the same situation could be described in other ways as well.

Please note that while addition is commutative, subtraction is usually not, so the order in which the terms are written makes a difference. For instance, $7 - 3$ is not equal to $3 - 7$.

(On page 85 of this book you will see that subtraction is also defined in terms of adding the inverse element for addition.)

The properties of addition and subtraction are not dependent on the way we write about them. For example, we may write addition and subtraction problems either vertically or horizontally:

$$5 + 8 = \square \text{ or } \begin{array}{r} 5 \\ + 8 \\ \hline \end{array}$$

Your child should know that either way is acceptable. The meaning is the same and both are read as 'five *plus* eight'. The sign '+' is properly read as 'plus' rather than 'and.' Using *and* instead of *plus* can be confusing in many situations, and therefore your child should learn to use the proper word from the beginning. (The proper sign for the word 'and' is '&' and *not* '+'.) Similarly, the sign '—' should be read as 'minus' and not as 'take-away'.

MULTIPLICATION

The laws for the multiplication of whole numbers and fractions are.

CLOSURE. Multiplication of numbers results in a number for an answer. Thus, $3 \times 2 = 6$ (all whole numbers).

2	2	2
6		

Similarly, $2/3 \times 4/5 = 8/15$ (each a fraction).

COMMUTATIVE. The order in which numbers are multiplied does not change the product. Thus: $5 \times 3 = 3 \times 5$.

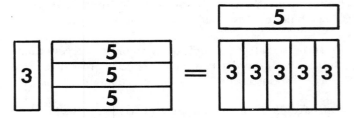

Try this with your rods and see if the rectangles are the same size.

(If your child remembers the product of 5 × 3 *but not 3 × 5, he will know from this law that the answers are the same.)*

Similarly, 2/3 × 4/5 = 4/5 × 2/3 = 8/15, and for the numbers a and b, a × b = b × a.

ASSOCIATIVE. Three numbers may be grouped in any combination for multiplication without changing the product. Thus:

$$2 \times (3 \times 5) = (2 \times 3) \times 5 \text{ or } 2 \times 15 = 6 \times 5 = 30$$

It does not matter which pair is multiplied first; the result is the same. Similarly, for the numbers a, b, and c, we can use the Cuisenaire rods to show that (a × b) × c = a × (b × c).

IDENTITY ELEMENT. For multiplication there is a special number—'one'—by which any other number may be multiplied without changing that other number. For any number 'a', 1 × a = a. One (1) is known as the identity element for multiplication For example. 1 × 13 = 13.

Division like subtraction is not considered an independent operation, but is defined in terms of multiplication. It is called the inverse operation to the operation of multiplication. You can think of division as undoing multiplication. For example, if you start with 8, then multiply by 4 and then divide by 4 you can see that dividing by 4 undoes the effect of multiplying by 4:

$$8 \times 4 \div 4 = 8. \ 8 \times (4 \div 4) = 8 \times 1 = 8$$

If you know that three times eight equals twenty-four, you can see that this relationship between the numbers can be expressed equally well as 3 × 8 = 24, 24 ÷ 8 = 3 or 24 ÷ 3 = 8. (Other variations on this are also possible, such as 8 × 3 = 24.)

Division is more thoroughly treated on Card G-5 and on page 71 of this book.

Multiplication is sometimes thought of as repeated addition, and division as repeated subtraction. Although this is (sometimes) helpful in learning how to do computations, you should know that in mathematics addition and multiplication are separate and independent operations which are connected together by the Distributive Law (see next section).

THE DISTRIBUTIVE LAW

How to Connect Multiplication with Addition (and Subtraction)

Some of the problems your child must face in mathematics will involve *both* addition and multiplication. Thus far we have dealt *separately* with these two operations. This was done to make clear the independent nature of these operations and to show their parallel structure, with the Fundamental Laws of Closure, Associativity, and Commutativity applying to each of them. Now we will show how these operations are connected through the Fundamental Law of Distribution. Much of the manipulative work in algebra and much of the computation in arithmetic is dependent on the use of this Law.

Your child should know not only how the Distributive Law is stated, but most importantly he should be able to apply it with facility. The suggestions for your child on creating his own equations (see page 42), for example, will be much more fun when he can consciously apply the Distributive Law.

The treatment of the Distributive Law here makes it easy for you to use the rods with your child in helping him to understand the Law. Since this section is for the adult, we can assume you already know the simple arithmetic used here. You will get the most out of it if you follow the examples, and use the rods yourself to see how the Law works.

The *Distributive Law* connects the two operations of multiplication and addition. This law, which enables you to distribute or spread multiplication across addition, states that if a, b, and c are numbers:

$a \times (b + c) = (a \times b) + (a \times c)$
If we let a = 5, b = 2, and c = 3, then,
$5 \times (2 + 3) = (5 \times 2) + (5 \times 3) + 10 + 15 = 25$
$5 \times 5 = 10 + 15 = 25$

The Cuisenaire rods show this as.

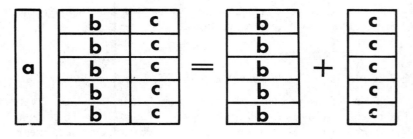

$$a \times (b + c) = (a \times b) + (a \times c)$$

Here is an example of the Distributive Law to work out with the rods: 5 × 7 = 35. Your child can represent the product (5 × 7) with the rods by crossing a yellow rod over a black rod. See Card G-4 *now* to be sure you understand this.

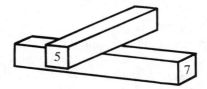

(A rectangle of five black rods will represent the result of 5 × 7.)

In the crossed rods above, the black rod can be replaced by a pair of rods equal to it in length, say *green plus purple*. Applying the Distributive Law, the multiplication is spread so that 5 × 7 or 5 × (3 + 4) becomes (5 × 3) + (5 × 4) without changing the product.

With the rods, it will look like this:

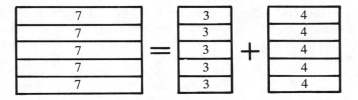

In numerals, the above looks like this:

$$5 \times 7 = 5 \times (3 + 4) = (5 \times 3) + (5 \times 4) = 15 + 20 = 35$$

The seven could also be replaced with some other equivalent expression such as $(1 + 6)$, $(2 + 5)$, $(10 - 3)$, etc. In the latter example, multiplication would be spread over subtraction:

$$5 \times 7 = 5 \times (10 - 3) = (5 \times 10) - (5 \times 3) = 50 - 15 = 35$$

The product in each case, when using an expression equivalent to seven, is always the same.

Whenever a number larger than ten is multiplied, the Distributive Law is always used. To find the product of 9×17, for example, you know that $17 = 10 + 7$. Thus:

$$9 \times 17 = 9 \times (10 + 7) = (9 \times 10) + (9 \times 7) = 90 + 63 = 153$$

Multiplication can be distributed even further. Thus, in the example 5×7, it was found that $5 \times 7 = 5 \times (3 + 4) = (5 \times 3) + (5 \times 4)$. The five can be replaced with an equivalent: $(2 + 3)$. Thus: $5 \times 7 = (2 + 3) \times (3 + 4)$. To distribute this, multiply each number in the first parentheses by each number in the second parentheses and add the results:

$$(2 \times 3) + (2 \times 4) + (3 \times 3) + (3 \times 4) = 6 + 8 + 9 + 12 = 35$$

This can be done easily with the Cuisenaire rods. The cross of the yellow and black rods (5×7), after being made into equivalents as above, ends up as crosses of. (red × green), (red × purple), (green

× green), and (green × purple). Have your child try this: make a train of 2 greens, 2 purples, 3 greens, and 3 purples. Add them all together and find the total in terms of white rods (use orange rods to find how many units of ten whites are in the total). It is easily seen, therefore, that the Distributive Law provides a way for a child to separate a new factor into two numbers which he can already multiply.

The Distributive Law is of great importance. Much of the trouble which pupils have results from their ignorance of this law. Your child will find this law helpful in working with multiplication of numbers larger than ten, understanding and using place value, and in learning the products used most often in multiplication. Understanding and mastery of it will be the key to how well and easily your child can do multiplication. The same law, incidentally, also applies to fractions.

ORDER OF OPERATIONS

Your child will be asked to solve problems where several operations are involved in the same problem. When parentheses are used (Card E-3B), there is no difficulty. Parentheses serve as grouping symbols and make clear the scope of a given operator. However, when there are no parentheses used, your child may not know which operations to perform first. You will often get a different answer if the operations are done in a different order. Here is an example of the difficulties that can arise: $4 + 12 \div 2 = ?$ If you did the addition first the answer is $(4 + 12) \div 2 = 8$, but if you do the division first the answer is $4 + (12 \div 2) = 10$. There are certain agreed-upon rules for proceeding with these cases. These suggest how parentheses might be placed.

When several or all of the fundamental operations of arithmetic (addition, subtraction, multiplication, and division) occur in succession, without parentheses being used, perform multiplications and divisions *before* additions and subtractions, and *in the order in which they occur,* from left to right. For example:

$$
\begin{aligned}
15 - 3 \times 6 \div 2 + 4 &= 15 - 18 \div 2 + 4 \text{ (result of multiplication)} \\
&= 15 - 9 + 4 \text{ (results of division)} \\
&= 6 + 4 \text{ (result of subtraction)} \\
&= 10 \text{ (result of addition)}
\end{aligned}
$$

The same result would have been achieved if parentheses had been used:

$$15 - (3 \times 6) \div 2 + 4 = 15 - (18 \div 2) + 4$$
$$= 15 - 9 + 4 \text{ etc.}$$

USING CORRECT MATHEMATICAL LANGUAGE

In addition to the words used in mathematics, a special set of symbols has been developed to express them. When you write an equation such as $(a + b)^2 = a^2 + 2ab + b^2$, it is an easier and simpler way for writing the following: "The square of a sum of two quantities is equal to the square of the first quantity plus twice the product of the second quantity times the first quantity plus the square of the second quantity." It is easier to see this clearly when it is expressed in a simple and appropriate notation. You and your child should recognize that the symbols in mathematical equations are essentially a form of shorthand for expressions in words.

English is essentially a phonetic language (not as much so as Spanish, Finnish, or Turkish). Some languages, such as Chinese, are character or sign languages in which a separate sign represents each word in the language. English, like Chinese, has many words which can be written with a single symbol or sign instead of several letters. Some examples are the words: plus, minus, times, equals, one, two, three, four, etc. Each of these words can be written with the appropriate sign: +, –, ×, =, 1, 2, 3, 4, etc.

You and your child should use consistently the correct English word which belongs with each of these signs. It is much easier for a young child to learn the correct words from the beginning. In doing so, he will avoid any unlearning or confusion later. The mathematical terms on the Activity Cards and in this book have been so chosen that your child will never be confused in high school or college by the need to unlearn terminology.

As your child develops a mathematical vocabulary, it will be useful for him to apply it to describe situations in the world around him. As he describes real or imaginary situations, he can make up "number stories" similar to the examples given on page 45.

HELPING YOUR CHILD CREATE MATHEMATICAL EQUATIONS

The typical workbook exercises that are found in many modern textbooks deliberately have not been included in this Cuisenaire Mathematics Study Kit. The activities in the Activity Cards of this Kit encourage your child to create his own examples and problems. Not only is this fun but it is also a most useful activity. All your child needs is a pencil or pen, some blank paper, and the Cuisenaire rods for checking his work.

After your child has completed the activities suggested on Card Series E, he is ready to create his own equations describing what he finds about numbers. Ask him to start by making equations using some specific number such as, for example, 8. He should try whatever comes into his mind, first writing the equation, then being allowed to check it with the rods *if he is not sure* he is right. However, do not always force your child to check every equation as this would make it drudgery instead of fun. The complexity of the equations will depend on how much he knows. A young child with little experience in arithmetic might make these.

$$5 + 3 = 8 \qquad 8 - 5 = 3 \qquad 2 + 6 = 8 \qquad 8 = 9 - 1$$

However, a child with more experience may create much more complex equations. Here are some stories about the number 8 invented by six-year-old children. They are reprinted from *Experiences With Numbers in Color* by Madeleine Goutard.

$$8 + 8 \times 1 = 4 \times 2 = 2 \times 4.$$

$$8 = 1/4 \times 32 = 1/5 \times 40 = 1/6 \times 48 = 8/30 \times 30 = 8/34 \times 34 = 1/2 \times 16 = 8/17 \times 17 = 8/19 \times 19 = 8/1 \times 1.$$

$$8 = 8/2 \times 1/2 \times 4 = 8/4 \times 1/2 \times 8 = 8/5 \times 1/2 \times 10 = 8/6 \times 1/2 \times 12.$$

$$8 = 8/119 \times (118 + 1) = 8/130 \times (129 + 1) = 8/100000 \times 100000 = 8/100 \times (99 + 1).$$

$$8 = 40 - (14 + 18) = 30 - (14 + 8) =$$
$$50 - (8 + 4 + 8 + 2 \times 5 + 3 \times 3 + 1 + 2) =$$
$$40 - (8 + 4 + 8 + 2 \times 5 + 2).$$

$$8 = 1/2 \times 14 + 10 - 9 = 1/6 \times 36 + 1/2 \times 4 = 1/3 \times 15 + 12 - 9 =$$
$$1/3 \times 12 + 8 - 4 = 1/2 \times 6 + 1/4 \times 20 = 1/3 \times 6 + 1/2 \times 12 =$$
$$1/2 \times 2 + 1/3 \times 21.$$

$$8 = 5 + 2 + 1 = 1 + 2 + 5 = 4 + 3 + 1 = 5 + 1 + 2 = 3 + 4 + 1 =$$
$$4 + 1 + 3 = 1 + 4 + 3 = 4 + 1 + 2 + 1 = 2 + 1 + 5 = 5 + 3 =$$
$$4 + 4 = 6 + 2 \times 1.$$

$$8 = 7/18 \times (10 + 8) + 12 \div 12 = 14 \div 2 + 1 + 3 - (1 + 2) =$$
$$10 - (1 + 1) = 8/19 \times (10 + 9) = 1 + 9 - (1 + 1) = 8/15 \times 15 =$$
$$1/3 \times 24 = 8/25 \times 25 = 1/4 \times 32 = 1/5 \times 40 = 1/6 \times 48 =$$
$$8/60 \times 60 = 10 - (2 \times 1) = 8 \times 1 = 1 \times 8 = 2 \times 4 = 4 \times 2 =$$
$$1 + 10 - (1 + 2) = 2 + 3 + 1 + 2 = 8/17 \times (10 + 7) = 1 + 3 + 1 + 2 + 1 =$$
$$5 + 1 + 2 = 8/16 \times 16 = 4/5 \times 10 = 8/1000 \times 10^3 = 8/1 \times 1 =$$
$$8 + 2 - (1 + 1) = 8/27 \times 27 = 8/3 \times 3 = 8/28 \times 28 = 8 + 4 - (1 + 3) =$$
$$11 - (1 + 1 + 2) \text{ (wrong)} = 8/90 \times 90 = 8/110 \times 110 = 8/113 \times 113 =$$
$$8/118 \times 118 = 8/114 \times 114 = 8/112 \times 112 = 8/117 \times 117 =$$
$$8/115 \times 115 = 8/111 \times 111.$$

The following is an example of how your child might start expanding an equation. (He will find his own special ways that are fun for him.) Suppose he happened to start by writing 7 = 3 + 4 (perhaps from something he has made with the rods or from something he happens to remember). The next step might be remembering that four is one-half of eight, so he expands his equation to 7 = 3 + 4 = 3 + (1/2 × 8). Perhaps he notices next that 3 = 12 - 9, so he replaces the 3 in his equation with the equivalent expression $(12 - 9)$, making it now $7 = 3 + 4 = 3 + (1/2 \times 8) = (12 - 9) + (1/2 \times 8)$. Since $12 = 2 \times 6$, the next step might be $(2 \times 6) - 9 + (1/2 \times 8) = 7$. This should not be done as a routine exercise, but should be an opportunity for your child to make his own discoveries and write about them.

The activities of Card G-1 on Equivalent Expressions will suggest many ways of creating the child's own mathematical equations. His understanding of the Distributive Law will make it easy for him to start with a simple equation and gradually expand it into a very complex statement.

As your child learns more about mathematical operations and gains more experience with number manipulations, he will create more and more complex equations. The insights he will gain in this way are much more useful in developing his mathematical skills than the benefits of doing exercises made by others. Your child will probably surprise you with some of the equations he creates!

SOLVING WORD PROBLEMS

Often your child will be asked to solve (or invent) problems stated in words, but involving mathematics for their solution. In this Cuisenaire Mathematics Study Kit, we have deliberately presented mathematical relationships first, often using the Cuisenaire rods as a model to help your child discover the meanings behind these relationships. This is much more efficient for the child than asking him to discover the rules of arithmetic from tricky problems. As he gains new knowledge and experience in mathematics, however, he will apply it to solving "word problems" or "story problems."

When a problem is stated in words, your child should first look for the mathematical relationships involved in the problem, and then write an equation (or several) to describe what he sees. If he has learned how the operations of mathematics are related to each other, he may see a choice of equations to describe the problem. For example:

"Your family is driving 100 miles to the beach for a picnic. You stopped for gas after going 20 miles. How much farther must you go?" This problem could be thought of in different ways and several different yet appropriate equations may be used to find the answer.

$$20 + \square = 100 \qquad 100 - 20 = \square \qquad (1/5 \times 100) + \square = 100$$

Solving any of these equations will provide the right answer. 80.

It is not necessary (or usually desirable) to insist that a given problem be thought of as a "subtraction problem" or an "addition problem." A child who *understands* what he has learned about mathematics will realize there may be several ways of looking at the same problem.

It is a very good exercise for your child to invent story problems as well as solve them. He should be allowed to use any numbers he chooses. You might start by asking him to tell you a story which uses numbers. Here are some stories made up by children which are reprinted from *Mathematics and Children* by Madeleine Goutard.

Lise, (7 years)

I have 80 paper dolls. They are all girls. I make 10 boys. There are not enough boys. I make another 5. How many dolls have I got now? Answer. 80 + 10 + 5 = 95

Suzanne, (7 years)

I go to school. I meet 23 boys. When I turned around, there were only 10. How many are gone?

Francis, (6 years)

There are 12 white police dogs at the station. My father who is a policeman buys 6 more brown ones and 6 big black ones. The station now has 24 dogs.

Daniel, (6 years)

Peter has the flu. He has 7 germs on his tongue and 5 in his nose. This makes 12 germs.

Marie, (7 years)

There was a woman who had 300 husbands in jail. They made a hole in the wall and they all came out. = 0 in the jail.

THE CONCEPT OF THE "SET"

Central to the mathematics which children learn in school is the *set* concept. A knowledge of sets can help your child get a better understanding of arithmetic and mathematics as a whole. The set concept appears in arithmetic, algebra, geometry, symbolic logic, and in all other divisions of higher mathematics. Thus, every new mathematical idea which your child learns, from kindergarten through college, is related to it. The word *set* therefore will be used in your child's homework, as well as in the Activity Cards of this Kit.

What is a *set?* A set is a well-defined collection of things or objects (called members or elements). The members belong to or are *contained* in the set. A *set* of chinaware is an example of a set. Each of the plates, cups, bowls, saucers, etc. is a member of your set of chinaware. You know whether or not a particular piece of chinaware belongs to your set.

A set is any well-defined group of objects. A collection of crayons is a set. So are the marbles in a marble-bag, or the beads on a necklace. A red crayon is a member of the set of crayons. A blue marble is a member of the set of marbles. The largest or center bead in the necklace is a member of the set of beads in the necklace.

Here are some other well-defined sets.

- The set of your parents and grandparents
- The set of former presidents of the United States
- The set of numbers greater than five
- The set of your child's classmates

A set can be described in writing in several ways. Here we shall describe the same set, Set A, in three ways. (1) By listing the names of each of the members of the set between braces and separated by commas. Set A = $\{a, b, c, d\}$. (2) By describing the qualifications for set membership. Set A is the set of all x such that x is a letter before e in the English alphabet. This would be written as Set A = $\{x \mid x:$ letter before e in the English alphabet$\}$. (The symbol $\mid$ is read as "such that".) (3) By describing Set A as the first four letters in

46

the English alphabet. All these are just different ways of naming the same thing. (In listing the members of a set the same members should not be listed twice. Thus {a, a, a, b, c, d} is not a correct listing because the member 'a' appears twice. {a, a, a} is defined as the set {a}, called the singleton of a.)

Two sets are *equal* (or identical) to each other if they have exactly the same members. The order in which they are listed does not matter. Thus {a, b. c. d} = {b, d. a. c} In this case each set has the same members and the same number of members. Two sets may be equal even though they have different names. Thus. the set of U.S. presidents is identical to the set of U.S. chief executives.

Two sets are *equivalent* to each other if the members can be matched, one for one. There need be no other similarity or relationship between the sets. The set of Justices of the U.S. Supreme Court is equivalent to the set of members of a baseball team in the field because each set contains the same number of members, even though the members are different. This property — equivalence — of sets is used in primary school grades to explain the ideas of numbers. If your child can match the members of two sets exactly, one-for-one, with none left over, the sets are equivalent. (Can he match his fingers exactly with his toes? Since he can, he knows that his set of toes is equivalent to his set of fingers, even if he doesn't know the number name 'ten'.) Equivalent sets will have the same *cardinal number* assigned to them.

Subsets are sets whose members are also members of another set. If every member of one set is also a member of a second set, the first set is a subset of the second, and we say the first set is included in the second. Thus. if Set A is included in Set B, we say Set A is a subset of Set B and we write it as "Set A ⊂ Set B" and read it as "Set A is a subset of (or — is included in) Set B." Similarly. the set {1, 2. 3} is a subset of the set {1, 2, 3, 4, 5}.

Set union and intersection are often shown by means of drawings called Venn diagrams as shown below.

In figure 1 the intersection of sets A and B is shaded.

In figure 2 the union of sets A and B is shaded.

The *complement* of set A in respect to set B is the set of all members of set A that are *not* members of set B. In figure 3 the complement of set A in respect to set B is shaded. This complement is also described as Set A – Set B.

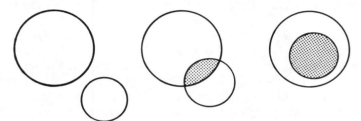

Figure 1

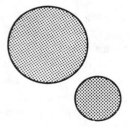
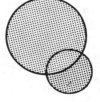

Figure 2

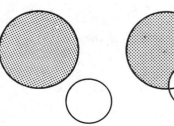

Figure 3

The *empty set,* also called the *null* set, is a special set with no members. It is a subset of every set. The set of grandfathers who are only ten years old is the empty set. it has no members. Similarly, the set of female presidents of the U.S. is the empty set, without members. There are two notation symbols for the empty set. one is a pair of braces with a blank space between: { } . The other is the symbol ϕ, without any braces. (Zero is the cardinal number of the empty set.)

A new set can be formed from any two sets. It is called the *union* set and contains every member that is either of the original two sets, without repeating any member. The symbol for union is ∪. The union of {1,2,3,4,5} and {3,4,5,6,7} would therefore be.

$$\{1, 2, 3, 4, 5, 6, 7\}$$

Another new set can be formed from two sets. It is called the *intersection* set and contains only those members that belong to both original sets. No member may be repeated. The symbol for intersection is ∩. The intersection of {1, 2, 3, 4, 5} and {3, 4, 5, 6, 7} would therefore be:

$$\{3, 4, 5\}$$

When two sets have no members in common, they are called disjoint sets and their intersection is the empty set. Thus, if Set A = {1, 2, 3} and Set B = {4, 5, 6}, the intersection would be shown as:

$$\text{Set A} \cap \text{Set B} = \phi = \{\ \}$$

ORDERED SETS.

The order in which the members of a set are listed can be most important and is a key to the understanding of many mathematical concepts. To show that order does matter, we write the names of the members of the set within parentheses ( ) instead of braces { } Thus, the set (3, 2, 1) is not the same as the set (1, 2, 3).

When ordered sets are formed with two members, we call such sets *ordered pairs.* (D, 4), for example, might be an ordered pair of coordinates for locating a town on a map. The first member of the pair is drawn from one set {A, B, C, D, E . . . etc.} and the second member from another set {1, 2, 3, 4, 5 . . . etc}. Such ordered pairs are used in map-making, geometry, fractions, and in many other ways.

You can form ordered pairs by choosing the members from different sets. thus, the first member of each pair from a set of first names, and the second member from a set of family names. A set of such ordered pairs, describing your family and your neighbor's family, might look like this. {(John, Smith), (Jane, Smith), (Robert, Smith), (Mary, Adams), (Fred, Adams), (Tom, Adams), (Susan, Adams)}. Two ordered pairs are equal when their first elements and their second elements are the same.

The first and second elements of ordered pairs can both be chosen from the same set. For example, suppose that three boys take turns riding on a tandem (two-seat) bicycle. What are the different partnerships they can form? (It is a different partnership when the boys on the front and back seats change places; one may be better at steering). This is easily shown by forming ordered pairs from the set of three boys. {Tom, Dick, Harry}. The possible partnerships are (Tom, Dick), (Tom, Harry), (Dick, Harry), (Dick, Tom), (Harry, Tom), (Harry, Dick). In this example both the first and second elements of the ordered pairs were drawn from the same set of boys. Who is on the front seat and who is on the back seat for each partnership is easily seen by looking at the ordered pairs; in each case the boy on the front seat is listed first.

MODULAR OR CLOCK ARITHMETIC

One topic often taught in today's mathematics produces such strange looking mathematical sentences as $2 + 2 \equiv 0$ or $3 \times 2 \equiv 2$. It is known as "clock arithmetic", modular arithmetic, or finite arithmetic. Modular arithmetic is great fun for children and is one of the ways in which they can easily explore mathematical relationships without needing to memorize first many so-called "number facts".

A familiar example of modular arithmetic is the clock you use every day. Only twelve numerals appear on its face; when the hands reach twelve o'clock, they start over again. To find a time six hours later than nine o'clock, you do not add 6 and 9 to get 15 o'clock. Instead, you use three of the six hours to get from nine to twelve o'clock and then use the remaining three hours to get to three o'clock. In this system, which we call *modulo twelve,* we can say that $6 + 9 \equiv 3$.

Another example of modular arithmetic is our system of seven days in the week. If you agree on Thursday to meet a friend ten days later, you know that this will be in (7 + 3) days or (Thursday plus three days) or on a Sunday. This is a *modulo seven* system.

In modular systems the particular system is indicated by the term *modulo* followed by the specific number. For example, modulo 4 is a system which has only four numbers: 0, 1, 2, and 3. Counting in this system is as follows: 0, 1, 2, 3, 0, 1, 2, 3, 0, 1, 2, 3, ... etc. If you are working in modulo 4, any number larger than 4 is said to be *congruent (mod 4)* to the number which remains after you have subtracted four as many times as possible from the first number. This is indicated with a mathematical symbol, a third bar in the equals sign ($\equiv$), which is read as "congruent to". For example, $13 \equiv$ (mod 4) since after you have subtracted 4 from 13 three times, the remainder is 1. $8 \equiv 0$ (mod 4) since after you have subtracted 4 twice from 8 the remainder is 0.

Another example of modular arithmetic is the system of "odd and even". This is equivalent to the arithmetic of mod 2. In this system the only numbers are 0 (even) and 1 (odd). When you say that an even plus an even is an even, it is the same as (or equivalent to) $0 + 0 \equiv 0$ (mod 2). To say that an odd plus an odd equals an even is equivalent to $1 + 1 \equiv 0$ (mod 2). The other possibility is an even plus an odd is an odd, or $0 + 1 \equiv 1$ (mod 2). The complete addition table for mod 2 is like this:

Mod 2 Addition

+	0	1
0	0	1
1	1	0

The above table gives all the possibilities obtainable in adding odd and even numbers.

It is easy to understand modular arithmetic if you use the Cuisenaire rods. For this example, you will use *mod 4*. The numbers in mod 4, as we said before, are 0, 1, 2, and 3. These are represented with the rods as follows: 0 is no length, 1 the length of the white rod, 2 the length of the red rod, and 3 the length of the green rod. The rule in this mod 4 system will be to subtract the length of a purple rod whenever possible in naming a length, and as many times as possible.

Try some addition in mod 4: $2 + 3 \equiv \square$ (mod 4). Add the length of a red rod (2) and a green rod (3). The train you have made is equivalent in length to the yellow rod (5). To name the length in mod 4, first subtract the length of a purple rod from the train. What is the remainder after doing so? It is the white rod which (see above) we call 1. Thus, $2 + 3 \equiv 1$ (mod 4).

You can develop an addition table for mod 4 which will look like this:

Mod 4 Addition

+	0	1	2	3
0	0	1	2	3
1	1	2	3	0
2	2	3	0	1
3	3	0	1	2

(The sum of any number in the top row plus any number in the left row—in modulo 4—is found at the intersection of the two rows. Thus, $3 + 3 \equiv 2$ (mod 4).)

In any modular system, the largest number is always one less than the modulus. For example, in mod 4 the largest number is 3. However, there are four numbers in this system since you always start with 0 as the first number. Similarly, in mod 12 there are twelve numbers of which the smallest is 0 and the largest is 11.

If you use the length of the white rod as the unit length when using the Cuisenaire rods for modular arithmetic, remember that you subtract the length of the modulus (whenever possible) as many times as possible in naming a length. Thus, in mod 12, to name a length larger than orange + white, first subtract the length orange + red as often as possible. The remaining length is then named in terms of the white rod.

CALCULATORS

There is no section on the use of the hand calculator in the Activity Cards of this Kit. However, calculators are becoming an integral part of work with mathematics for everyone, both student and adult. Improved in operation and reduced in cost, calculators are now available universally to remove the drudgery from mathematical computation. Some of the fanciest now permit calculations which, a few years ago, would have been feasible only with a very large computer!

There is no question about whether children will use calculators. They are already doing so, both in the school and in the home. The hand calculator is now recommended for student use in colleges and high schools throughout the U.S., and is being adopted rapidly in Junior High and elementary school grades. A talking calculator has already been built for use by blind students! The most important question to ask and answer about calculators today is: "How do I use a calculator to make me better at understanding mathematics and more efficient at doing computations?"

The calculator enables one to put the emphasis on understanding *what* to do and how to do it, in the right sequence. Problem solving is the key to the effective use of the calculator. When the problem is understood and laid out appropriately, the calculations become a matter of merely pushing the proper buttons accurately. Mental approximation of answers becomes important so that you can recognize a wrong answer when you see it. A calculator will always give the right answer to the problem you feed into it. If you push the wrong keys, it will not answer the problem you want solved!

It is very desirable for your child to have a calculator for use at home. As soon as he is able to read numbers, he is ready to use the calculator to explore them. For example, by starting with the number "1", and adding "1" repeatedly, the student will find the sequence of the counting numbers, at a very early age level. The calculator can be very helpful with homework in several ways. First, it provides a way of checking answers after the pencil-and-paper work has been done. This enables your child to find and correct computational mistakes he may have made. Another way is to use the calculator initially to find the solutions to problems. When the calculator is used in this way, it is important to write down all the steps in the process, and the intermediate steps, not just the final answer. In this way, the mathematical processes become clear; the calculator does not "do the homework", but merely does the drudgery part of the computations. You, as parent or teacher, will have your own rules on how a calculator may be used by your child.

There are several simple hints to be observed in acquiring and using a calculator.

First, in selecting and buying a calculator, be sure to get one with algebraic logic, and with a four or five key memory. The light-emitting display should be either a bright green, or the new liquid crystal display of black on a white or yellow background. The latter type of display uses very little power and has such a long battery life that there is no need for an AC adaptor.

Second, read a good book on the use of the calculator. Several entertaining and instructive books are listed below and in the Bibliography (page 87)

2, 4, 6, 8, Let's Start to Calculate, by Jessica Davidson, offers a variety of suggestions on the use of calculators to enhance mathematical learning, to provide insights into the structure of numbers, and to arouse interest in the exploration and discovery of mathematical concepts. (Grades 4 through 9).

Boggle, by James Vine, uses simple words which can be made on a calculator, both to explore mathematical ideas, and to have fun!

Games, Tricks, and Puzzles, by Norman Pallas, emphasizes problem solving with the calculator over a wide grade range.

Calculator Explorations, by Don Miller, provides secondary students with considerable experience in using the calculator to solve real mathematical problems.

All of the above books are available from the publisher of this Kit.

THE METRIC SYSTEM OF MEASUREMENT

The metric system of measurement was developed by French scientists to measure lengths, distances, weights, volumes, and other values by a standard method. France adopted it as the legal system of measurement in 1799 and made it compulsory in 1837. By 1800, other European countries had adopted the metric system, thus replacing all prevailing units of measure, which varied from country to country.

By 1785, Thomas Jefferson in the United States used his knowledge of the metric system to devise the dollar and its decimal subdivisions of dimes (deci-), cents (centi-), and mills (milli-) to replace the hodgepodge of currencies then in use among the American colonies. Today, every major country in the world, except the U.S., is using the metric system exclusively or is in the last years of a legislated changeover. The use of the metric system of measurement was legalized in the U.S. in 1866. The Federal government is now encouraging us to join the rest of the world in shifting over. Many major industries have already made the changeover—such as pharmaceutical, automotive, NASA, etc. Some states have specified dates by which all school instruction shall use metric rather than English system units of measurement. (England made the changeover in 1965).

Your children will be living in a completely metric world in the near future, a change to which they are now adapting very easily. It is a little more difficult for those of us who have learned about the metric system relatively late in life! It is important for you to gain some familiarity with the metric system so that you too can make the transition smoothly and feel at ease with it!

The metric system is easy to learn and use. All units have a uniform scale of relation, based on the decimal system. Calculations are simple. The basic unit is the metre, the unit of length. The scale of multiples and subdivisions of the metre is ten. All units of area, volume, capacity, and weight are derived directly from the metre. The units for different kinds of measure are simply interrelated.

It is easy to change from one unit to another. Thus, to change from centimetres to kilometres, divide by 100,000. To change from millimetres to centimetres, divide by 10. To change from metres to centimetres, multiply by 100. By contrast, in the English system, to change from feet to miles, divide by 5,280. To change yards to inches, multiply by 36. To change inches to miles, divide first by 12 and then again by 5,280. You can see how much simpler the metric system is in terms of computational arithmetic!

HOW TO MASTER THE METRIC SYSTEM

1. *Think metric!* Don't waste time and effort converting to traditional units and back again. Do all estimating and measuring directly in metric units. By doing so, it will be faster and easier for you to become a metric expert!

2. *Estimate in metric before you measure!* Before you make a measurement, estimate how much it will be. Write down your estimate before you measure so that you can compare afterward.

3. *Measure many real objects!* Only through hands-on experience can you gain the facility with metric measurement which you need. Estimating, measuring, and calculating in the metric system is so much easier than in our customary system of English units that it is well worth the effort to learn!

METRIC LENGTH

The unit for length is the *metre*. This is about the length of a baseball bat. Historically, the metre was first established by calculating the earth's circumference at a given parallel and dividing the total by 40,000,000. The standard actually was recognized as the distance between two scratches on a platinum-iridium alloy bar kept in the International Bureau of Weights and Measures at Sevres, France, a suburb of Paris. In 1960, the metre was defined in terms of the wavelength of the orange-red line of the gas krypton-86 (about the color of the orange Cuisenaire rod).

METRIC AREA

The units for area are derived from those for length. Thus, a square metre (m^2) is a square measuring one metre long on each side. A square centimetre (cm^2) is a square measuring one centimetre long on each side.

METRIC VOLUME

The units for volume are derived similarly from those for length. A cubic metre (1 m^3) is a cube measuring one metre on each edge. A cubic centimetre (1 cm^3) is a cube measuring one centimetre on each edge. A simple way to visualize the latter is to look at a white Cuisenaire rod. The length of one edge is one centimetre (1 cm). The area of one face is one square centimetre (1 cm^2). The volume of the entire rod or cube is one cubic centimetre (1 cm^3).

METRIC CAPACITY

It is convenient to have a measure of how much a container can hold. For this purpose, the unit of a *litre* is used. One litre is the same amount of material as one thousand cubic centimetres. A litre is about the same measure of capacity as a quart.

METRIC WEIGHT OR MASS

The unit of weight is one *gram* (about half the weight of a dime or one-fifth the weight of a nickle). If a white rod were made of water, it would weigh one gram.

METRIC NAMES

Learning the names used in the metric system is very simple. There is one word each for length, weight, and capacity, and a set of prefixes which applies to all three words. For length the word is *metre* (sometimes spelled as *meter* in the U.S.); for weight the word is *gram*; for liquid capacity the word is *litre*. The prefixes are multiples or subdivisions by ten, as shown in the following table.

mega	=	multiply by 1,000,000
kilo-	=	multiply by 1,000
hecto-	=	multiply by 100
deka-	=	multiply by 10
UNIT	=	multiply by 1 , or leave unchanged (metre, litre, gram or second)
deci-	=	divide by 10
centi-	=	divide by 100
milli-	=	divide by 1,000
micro	=	divide by 1,000,000

There are other multiples and subdivisions used, chiefly in science, for very large or very small quantities. These need not be learned unless necessary. Some of the prefixes, such as deka- and hecto-, are used rarely.

TABLE OF METRIC UNITS AND ABBREVIATIONS

(with English equivalents)

LENGTH

Millimetre (mm) = 0.001 metres = 0.039 inch
Centimetre (cm) = 0.01 metre = 0.393 inch
Metre (m) = 1.000 metre = 39.37 inches =
    3.281 feet = 1.093 yards
Kilometre (km) = 1,000 metres = 0.621 mile = 3,281 feet

Inch (in) = 2.54 centimetres
Foot (ft) = 30.48 centimetres
Yard (yd) = 91.44 centimetres
Mile = 1.609 kilometres

AREA

Square centimetre (cm^2) = 0.155 square inch
Square metre (m^2) = 10.764 square feet = 1.196 square yards
Square kilometre (km^2) = 0.386 square mile
Hectare (ha) = 10,000 square metres = 2.471 acres

Square mile = 2.59 square kilometres

VOLUME

Cubic centimetre (cm^3) = 0.061 cubic inch
Litre (l) = 61.02 cubic inches = 1.057 quarts
Cubic metre (m^3) = 35.316 cubic feet

Quart (qt) = 0.946 litres
Gallon (gal) = 3.785 litres

WEIGHT

Milligram (mg) = 0.001 gram
Gram (g) = 0.035 ounce
Kilogram (kg) = 2.205 pounds

Ounce (oz) = 28.35 grams
Pound (lb) = 0.454 kilogram

IV

IF YOUR CHILD IS HAVING
DIFFICULTY WITH MATHEMATICS

IF YOUR CHILD IS HAVING DIFFICULTY LEARNING TO COUNT

Through the repetition of counting-out rhymes, and with help from parents, brothers, sisters, and by watching and listening to "Sesame Street" on TV, your child learns the rote sequence of counting number names- one, two, three, four . . . up to ten — usually before entering school. If your child has not developed this skill, introduce him to the variety of counting and number books at your local public children's library. Many of these colorful books present animals in their natural surroundings, with delightful texts to accompany them in which number is the primary theme. Read these books to your child and count along with him!

Give your child experience in counting small objects such as buttons, stones, crayons, bottle caps, marbles, clothespins . . . or Cuisenaire rods! For example:

Place two different colored rods in front of him. Count by touching each rod once, in sequence. Repeat several times. Add another rod and repeat the counting procedure several times. Rearrange the position of the rods so that the order is changed, and repeat the counting. Over a period of time, keep adding other rods until there are ten rods. Count slowly from left to right, touching each rod as you count. Rearrange the rods frequently to prevent the child from thinking that the number name belongs to a particular rod.

After demonstrating the above procedure, let your child try to count while you guide his hand in touching the rods. Let him count and touch at the same time, on his own. Keep the rods well-spaced from each other. When your child has learned to count and touch up to ten, give him a new task. pick up each rod as it is counted and place it in a pile. Start with a few rods and work up to ten. Ask him how many rods are in the pile. Get him to pick them up from the pile, one by one, and count them.

When the above has been mastered, ask him to count out a specified number of rods from a set of rods. Let him count until he reaches the specified number of rods and stops.

The game of DOMODOTS gives excellent experience in a special kind of matching which is involved in the development of counting skills. This game uses a random positioning of white and black dots on each playing tile so that no number pattern is present and connot be used to recognize a number concept. In order to match tiles, the child is forced to count the dots on each tile. He learns quickly that the concept of "how many" does not depend on how objects are arranged.

OVERCOMING TROUBLES WITH MATHEMATICS

Children's troubles with mathematics are often due to a lack of understanding of the basic ways in which numbers are related to each other. If your child is having difficulty with a specific problem, it is usually best to be sure first that he feels competent about the underlying essentials of how numbers work. He may need only a little help from you about something that was not clear to him; more often it is worth the time and effort to make sure of his fundamental understanding of mathematics. The farther he advances in mathematics by memorizing rules without understanding their meaning and why they work, the greater the difficulties he will face.

The suggestions which follow in this general section will be of help no matter what specific area of mathematics is giving your child difficulty. Later sections will deal in detail with specific areas of difficulties with number work.

It is important for your child to realize that most problems in mathematics can be solved from a few general rules, without memorizing many separate arbitrary facts and instructions. These rules are discussed in detail under the specific areas of possible difficulty. They are easy to remember and use; they are the axioms or postulates upon which our system of numbers is built.

Troubles often develop from the ways in which notation is used to describe in writing what we do with numbers. Mathematical notation and language and the sequence in which they are taught has come down to us through history. They are not always as clear as the ideas which they convey. The numbers which your child uses are related to each other, and it is these relationships that he must study. Your child should know that numbers are inter-related in several ways and that there are usually several alternate ways in which he can find the answer to a problem. Willingness to reason, not just to work by rote, is an essential to his good work in mathematics.

The activities on Activity Card Series B and E should be a good introduction to thinking about number relationships. These activities help your child to think about a relationship in more than one way. He learns to *think* about numbers and does not merely memorize "facts" about numbers. Although only numbers up to ten are described, the fundamental operations of arithmetic are introduced and related to each other in these particular Series (B and E).

Be sure that your child has a firm understanding of how our system of describing numbers to the base ten (decimal notation) works. (This is covered on pages 30 and 31 of this Guidebook, and in Series I of the Activity Cards.) He will learn that notation is only a help to him and that the most valuable tool he will use to solve problems in arithmetic is his brain! Pencil, paper, Cuisenaire rods, calculators, etc.—all are only aids to his mind. Your child must be a master of notation, not its slave!

IF YOUR CHILD IS HAVING DIFFICULTY
WITH ADDITION AND SUBTRACTION

ADDITION. If your child is having trouble with the addition of two numbers which add up to less than twenty, he probably has not learned the sequence of number names, and the patterns of numbers. For this the exercises on Activity Card E-3A should help him. He also should do a variety of addition problems, using the rods only for checking his answers after they have been written. This will help him to become confident when he is right and to pinpoint what he has not learned well.

Your child may have a lack of understanding of the place value system. If he is to work with numbers larger than 9, such as 27 or 325, he must understand how to write numbers. For this the exercises on Activity Card E-5 will be helpful. He should know that he can do a sum like

$$287$$
$$+\ 355$$

by the usual way of adding the units, then proceeding to the tens column, adding them, then going to the hundreds column and adding them. It may be helpful at first to rewrite the original sums to show what place value means. (This uses the associative and commutative laws described on pages 33-34 of this Guidebook.)

$$287 = 200 + 80 + 7$$
$$355 = 300 + 50 + 5$$
$$500 + 130 + 12 = 500 + 100 + 30 + 10 + 2$$
$$= 600 + 40 + 2 = 642$$

It will be helpful for your child to work out a few sums this long way so that he understands one way to get the right answer. Then he should do the exercises of Activity Card I-5 to see how we proceed by adding the units column, writing the answer of how many units, writing the number of tens to be added to the tens column, adding this, carrying if necessary to the hundreds column, etc.

SUBTRACTION: If your child is having trouble with subtraction, he may not understand what subtraction is, or he may be having trouble because some subtraction problems look easier than others. (For example, 203 – 200 may look easier than 201 – 198; both examples are equally easy. See Card G-3.)

It is important for your child to know that subtraction undoes addition, that it is not an independent, separate operation but merely another way of looking at a problem thought of in terms of addition. (See Activity Card A-5.) Thus, 43 – 18 = □ is another way of stating the same relationship as 18 + □ = 43. It is most important that your child recognize that subtraction and addition are inverses of each other, or opposite faces of the same coin.

The notation above — (43 – 18) can also be considered as a numeral that names a number. We usually write 25 as the standard name for this number. Your child should know that in today's mathematics programs there are several right and acceptable ways of writing and solving this kind of problem. When you (the adult) were studying subtraction in school, you probably were taught to "borrow" or "regroup". Sometimes subtraction is still taught with the use of the term "borrowing". However, there are other and better ways of finding the answer to a problem involving subtraction.

Activity Cards G-2, 3 provide a good approach to understanding the ways in which a subtraction problem may be handled. The key to many of the ways of changing a "difficult"-looking subtraction problem to an easy one involves adding zero. From basic arithmetic laws previously discussed, you already know that adding zero does not change a number. Thus, if 2 is added to each part of the expression (43 – 18) to form (45 – 20), you have really added (2 – 2), which is just another name for zero!

Although regrouping or borrowing is not the best way to teach subtraction the child's teacher may wish him to learn in this way. If so, the Cuisenaire rods will make it easier for him to understand how "borrowing" or "regrouping" works.

First, your child must understand place value by using Activity Cards I-1, 5. Take the numeral 387 as an example. The digits refer to.

hundreds	tens	units or ones
3	8	7

This can be shown in writing as: (300) + (80) + (70 = 387. If your child knows that 387 = (3 × 10 × 10) + (8 × 10) + (7), which can be represented with the rods, he is ready for the next step:

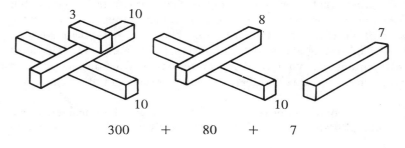

$$300 \quad + \quad 80 \quad + \quad 7$$

He can move one ten from the (8 × 10), leaving (7 × 10), and place this ten with the seven. He has only regrouped his rods, not changed the number.

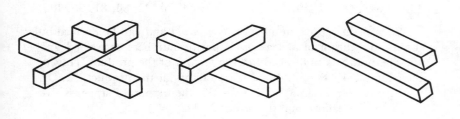

300   +   70   +   17   =   387

To subtract 39 is now easy.

300 + (70 − 30) + (17 − 9) = 300 + 40 + 8 = 348

Your child can always rewrite the name of a number so that he is subtracting a smaller number from a larger. The term "borrowing" is therefore not correct; there is no "paying back" involved!

Left-to-right subtraction can also be used to get the answer to a subtraction problem. It is described on Activity Card G-3. Although this method is not good for teaching mathematical understanding, is is easy to do and does not make subtraction problems appear "easy" or "difficult." They all become easy!

IF YOUR CHILD IS HAVING DIFFICULTY WITH MULTIPLICATION . . .

I. *He Doesn't Know His Multiplication Facts?*

There are ways by which learning of products in multiplication tables is made more interesting and which also help your child improve his general mathematical skills at the same time. Your child can learn the products of numbers up to at least ten times ten without enduring the drudgery of memorizing by rote.

There are 37 numbers between 1 and 100 whose properties can be investigated by your child to provide all the "multiplication facts" he needs. These numbers are:
4, 6, 8, 9, 10, 12, 14, 15, 16, 18, 20, 21, 24, 25, 27, 28, 30, 32, 35, 36, 40, 42, 45, 48, 49, 50, 54, 56, 60, 63, 64, 70, 72, 80, 81, 90, 100.

Each of the above numbers is a *product* and can be derived by the multiplication of at least two specific numbers between 1 and 10. The numbers multiplied are the *factors* of the product. Thus in the example 4 × 8 = 32, 4 and 8 are factors of the product, 32. Or, in the example 2 × 2 × 2 × 2 × 2 = 32, the numeral 2 appears five times in the factors of the product 32.

On Activity Card F-3, your child will find suggestions which show him how he can start with a multiplication such as 4 × 8 and find for himself what number this names. He will also learn how to work back from the number (product) and find its factors (which may be more than one pair).

A variety of inter-related games will fix the multiplication factors and product firmly in your child's mind while he is having fun. Take one or more of the above numbers each day and ask your child to form each number's length with the Cuisenaire rods, using the white rod as the unit and using as many orange rods as possible.

Let's say you select the number 12. Your child makes a train of 12 white rods. Now ask him to make this same length with as many trains of other colors as he can, each train being just as long as the 12 white rods. He may develop a pattern such as this:

1	1	1	1	1	1	1	1	1	1	1	1
2		2		2		2		2		2	
3			3			3			3		
4				4				4			
6						6					
10										2	

Factors of 12.
(12 × 1)   (3 × 4)
(6 × 2)   (2 × 6)
(4 × 3)

Your child can name the trains in terms of number factors: 12×1, 6×2, 4×3, 3×4, 2×6. He will learn, too, that the orange rod substitutes for ten white rods, thus making it easy for him to construct and properly name numbers larger than ten. From the above factors, you can ask your child questions as $2 \times 6 = ?$, $1/2 \times 12 = ?$, $1/3 \times 12 = ?$, $4 \times 3 = ?$, etc. In answering your questions, he will find that interrelated facts about the number 12 are easier for him to remember than memorizing multiplication tables. He may also discover other interesting information about number factors: for example, there is sometimes an even, sometimes an odd number of trains, depending on whether the product is a perfect square or not. For example, the factor "trains" of 16 (a perfect square) are: (16×1), (8×2), (4×4), (2×8)—a total of four trains (an even number). For 18 (not a perfect square), the factor "trains" are: (18×1), (9×2), (2×9), (3×6), (6×3)—a total of five trains (an odd number).

II. *He Doesn't Remember Products?*

It is easy for your child to find a product he doesn't remember *if* he thoroughly understands the important fundamental number laws about multiplication. They are stated formally on pages 35-37.

The *commutative law* tells your child that the order in which two numbers are multiplied does not matter, that 7×9 *must* give the same result as 9×7. He can see this easily by working out a few examples with the Cuisenaire rods. (See example on page 36.) Thus, if he is asked for the answer to 3×9 but he only remembers 9×3, he will be confident that the answers to both are the same.

The *distributive law* makes it easy for your child to find a product he doesn't remember by changing the problem to use products he does remember. This law tells your child that he can spread a multiplication across a sum. (See pages 37-40.)

Suppose he does not remember 6×7. If he remembers 6×5, he can start from there: $5 + 2 = 7$. Therefore, he can state that $6 \times 7 = 6 \times (5 + 2)$. The distributive law tells him that $6 \times (5 + 2) = (6 \times 5) + (6 \times 2) = 30 + 12 = 42 = 6 \times 7$. Your child might remember some other product; the principle still works. If he remembers 6×8, he could write the problem using $(8 - 1) = 7$. Thus:

$$6 \times 7 = 6 \times (8 - 1) = (6 \times 1) = 48 - 6 = 42.$$

Eventually your child will know all the products for the numbers 1 to 10 and some others beyond these. But it is good for his mathematical confidence and competence to *know* that he can find a product he has not yet learned by following the basic laws of multiplication.

III. *He Has Trouble With Several-Digit Multiplication?*

The key to this problem is an understanding of the *distributive law*. If your child has difficulty with problems such as 24 × 347, check first his knowledge of multiplication products up to 10 × 10 (covered in previous section). Be sure he knows what is meant by place value (see Card I-1). If he understands these fundamental principles, he can then apply the distributive law to get the answer to 24 × 347.

It may help your child to write 24 × 347 in a different way, like this.

$$(20 + 4) \times (300 + 40 + 7)$$

Then he can multiply each of the numbers in the second parentheses by the 20 in the first parentheses, then multiply the same numbers again by the 4 in the first parentheses. All products are then added together.

$$(20 \times 300) + (20 \times 40) + (20 \times 7) +$$
$$(4 \times 300) + (4 \times 40) + (4 \times 7) =$$
$$6000 + 800 + 140 + 1200 + 160 + 28 = 8,328$$

Your child should do several examples like the above, in full. Only then should he try the abbreviated method of writing and completing the problem in the usual, familiar way.

$$\begin{array}{r} 347 \\ \times\ \ 24 \\ \hline 1388 \\ 6940 \\ \hline 8328 \end{array}$$

(The above is only a "shorthand" way of writing; the meaning of handling the problem by applying the distributive law should be clear first, otherwise your child may become confused.)

When your child gets to know the distributive law well, he can find many shortcuts that will make it possible for him to do some multiplication problems more quickly. For instance, this law makes it easy to find the answer to 299 × 423.

$$299 \times 423 = (300 - 1) \times 423 = 126,900 - 423 = 126,477.$$

Your child is likely to be better than you at finding and understanding such shortcuts. Remember that the distributive law is the key to mastering multiplication!

IF YOUR CHILD IS HAVING DIFFICULTY WITH DIVISION

What is division? In one sense, division is the inverse or the undoing of multiplication. However, if your child doesn't really understand this, he may find it most helpful to think of division as repeated subtraction.

The basic equation for solving division problems is:

$$N = d \times q + r$$

In this equation, N is the number to be divided (called the dividend), d is the number by which the dividend is divided (called the divisor), q is the number of times d can be subtracted from N, and r is the remainder or what is left over after you have subtracted d × q from N.

An example will make this equation clear. divide 247 by 24, or 247 ÷ 24. N in the above equation is 247 and d is 24, so you can rewrite the problem as 247 = 24 × q + r. It is easy to guess 10 as a value for q, since you know that 24 × 10 = 240. If you try 10 as a value for q, you get 247 = 24 × 10 + r or 247 = 240 + r, so r must be 7. Now you have solved the whole problem. 247 = 24 × 10 + 7, which can also be written as 247 ÷ 24 = 10 remainder 7. The remainder r should be a number smaller than d.

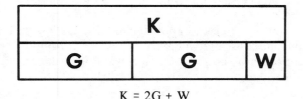

K = 2G + W

In the above drawing, the black rod K is N (the number to be divided) and the green rod G is d (the number by which N is to be divided). It is easily apparent in the above example that Q, the number of times you can subtract G from K, is equal to two. The remainder, r, is the white rod W. Using the white rod as the unit, the above example could be expressed in numbers as:

$$7 = (2 \times 3) + 1 \text{ or } 7 \div 3 = 2, \text{remainder } 1$$

Your child can always solve a division problem by: (1) subtracting again and again the number by which he wishes to divide until he can't subtract any more, and (2) then adding up how many times he did this to get the answer. This will certainly work but it is so tedious that easier ways to divide have been developed. It will be well, however, for your child to solve several division problems by repeated subtraction so that he is sure it works! Here are two examples for him.

$$56 \div 17 \qquad 345 \div 58$$

For many years, schools in France have been teaching a new method of division. It has been so successful that it has been adopted for most of the mathematics program textbooks in the U.S. It involves the distributive law and the use of repeated subtraction.

From the distributive law we know that if 980 = 28 × 35, it also could be expressed as 980 = 28 × (20 + 15) = 28 × (17 + 18) = 28 × (30 + 5). Thus:

$$980 \div 28 = 35 = 20 + 15 = 17 + 18 = 30 + 5, \text{etc.}$$

This basic mathematical law thus provides a key to a way of performing division—the method used in French schools—that enables your child to use profitably whatever guesses or estimates he makes in performing division. The following example— 980÷28 shows how to proceed with the notation in performing division by this new method.

The problem is set up like this: The space to the right of the vertical line is for trial divisors or estimates. Suppose you first guess that 28 can be subtracted 20 times. Write the 20 to the right of the line, multiply 20 × 28 to get 560 and subtract this form 980. The balance is 420. You can certainly subtract 28 another ten times, so write 10 to the right, multiply it to get 280, then subtract it from the 420. The balance is now 140. Suppose

```
28 ) 980      20
      560
      420      10
      280
      140       4
      112
       28       1
       28
            |  35
```

you guess that 28 can be subtracted four more time from 140. Try the 4, multiply it to get 112. You now find the remainder is 28. Finally, you put a 1 to the right to show that 28 can be subtracted once more. Now add up the number to the right of the vertical line and you get 35. This can be checked by multiplying 28 × 35 = 980. If you had made other guesses, it would not have mattered, except to make the problem a little faster or slower to solve, depending on how good your guesses were. The important thing is that you work each time with a smaller number and get closer and closer to the final answer.

Ask your child to try the following problems by this new method.

3251 ÷ 58   43,257 ÷ 847   845,867 ÷ 39

When your child has gained even more knowledge about mathematics, he can extend this system so that he can also make use of estimates that are too large. This can be done by the use of negative numbers. In the above example, note what would have happened if the first estimate had been 40 instead of 20.

```
28 ) 980      40
     1120
    − 140     − 5
    − 140    |  35
```

$40 \times 28 = 1120$. If you subtract 1120 from 980, the result is -140. 28 divides into 140 five times but since it is -140, you must write -5 to the right. Since there is no further remainder, you simply add

40 and − 5 to get 35. Or, if you prefer, think of it as adding 40 and subtracting 5. In any case, the answer is 35 and you did not need to throw away your first estimate and start over.

IF YOUR CHILD IS HAVING
DIFFICULTY WITH FRACTIONS

A few simple, basic principles will help your child understand and use fractions. First, a fraction is essentially a *ratio* involving two numbers. Second, fractions are numbers (we call them *rational* numbers) which have all the fundamental number properties or laws of whole numbers and integers as well as a few new ones of their own.

The numerals for fractions can be written in several ways. One-fifth can be written as $1/5$, $\frac{1}{5}$ or $(1, 5)$. The "1" in each example is called the first member (or numerator) and the "5" is the second member (or denominator) of the pair of numbers used to name this fraction. Whole numbers are a special kind of fraction whose second member is one. Thus, the whole number 5 is also the fraction $5/1$. No fraction can have "0" as a first member.

For every fraction there is another fraction, called its inverse or reciprocal, which can be formed by exchanging the first and second members with each other. Thus, the reciprocal of $1/5$ or $(1, 5)$ is $5/1$ or $(5, 1)$. (The inverse or reciprocal of a fraction is therefore that number by which the fraction can be multiplied to produce 1. Thus: $1/5 \times 5/1 = 1$.)

(The activities on Activity Card H-1 make clear the simple relationship between a unit fraction like $1/7$ and a fraction like $7/1$.)

The fraction 1/7 looks like this with the Cuisenaire rods:

The inverse or reciprocal of 1/7 is 7/1 which looks like this:

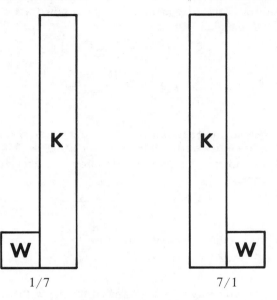

Just as with whole numbers, there are many different equivalent names for fractions. (See Card H-2). For example: 2/3 = 20/30 = 40/60 = 400/600 = 12/18 = 24/36 = etc. The Cuisenaire rods make clear the various names for the fraction 2/3:

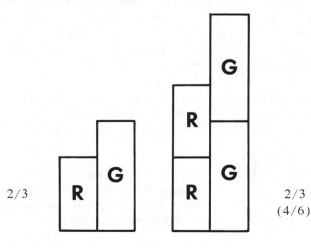

ADDITION (OR SUBTRACTION). If the second members of each of two fractions being added (or subtracted) are the same, add (or subtract) the first members to get a new fraction with the same second member. Thus:

$$5/3 + 8/3 = \frac{5 + 8}{3} = 13/3$$

$$17/24 - 9/24 = \frac{17 - 9}{24} = 8/24$$

If the second members are not the same, change one or both fractions into equivalent fractions with the same second members, then add (or subtract) to get a new fraction with the same second member. Thus:

$$8/3 + 5/7 = \frac{7 \times 8}{7 \times 3} + \frac{3 \times 5}{3 \times 7}$$

Since the second members are now the same, proceed to:

$$8/3 + 5/7 = 56/21 + 15/21 = (56 + 15)/21 = 71/21$$

Sometimes you may need to change only one of the fractions to an equivalent form. For example:

$$2/3 + 5/6 = 4/6 + 5/6 = (4 + 5)/6 = 9/6 = 3/2$$

The smallest number that will serve as the second member for adding (or subtracting) fractions is called the lowest common denominator. It is known as the lowest common multiple of the two second members. However, you do not need to memorize these definitions in order to work with fractions.

(Note. All rules presented here regarding fractions apply also to whole numbers. Whole numbers are special fractions whose second members are always 1. Thus: 5 + 8 = 13 could also be written as: 5/1 + 8/1 = (5 + 8)/1 = 13/1.)

MULTIPLICATION. To find the new fraction equivalent to the multiplication of two fractions, multiply the first members together to form the new first member, then multiply the second members together to form the new second member. Expressed in another way. multiply the numerators to get the numerator of the product, and multiply the denominators to get the denominator of the product. Thus:

$$3/5 \times 2/7 = (3 \times 2)/(5 \times 7) = 6/35$$
$$17/2 \times 4/3 = (17 \times 4)/(2 \times 3) = 68/6 = 34/3$$

This rule also applies to whole numbers (special fractions).

$$4 \times 5 = 4/1 \times 5/1 = (4 \times 5)/(1 \times 1) = 20/1$$

Fractions and whole numbers, therefore, work in the same way.

DIVISION. We have discussed earlier the fact that the operations of multiplication and division are inverses or reciprocals of each other; each undoes the other.

$24 \div 6$ is the same as $24 \times 1/6$. In this example, $6/1$ and $1/6$ are reciprocals of each other. Dividing by a number or multiplying by the reciprocal of that number produces the same result.

To divide one fraction by another, therefore, is the same as multiplying one fraction by the reciprocal of the other. Thus:

$$24/1 \div 6/1 = 24/1 \times 1/6 = \frac{24 \times 1}{1 \times 6} = 24/6 = 4/1$$

$$2/3 \div 4/5 = 2/3 \times 5/4 = \frac{2 \times 5}{3 \times 4} = 10/12 = 5/6$$

$$5/3 \div 2/7 = 5/3 \times 7/2 = \frac{5 \times 7}{3 \times 2} = 35/6$$

PERCENTAGE

Percentage is fundamentally a special language and notation for certain ratios or fractions. It is sometimes taught in school as though it were a special topic in mathematics, which can be most confusing to the student. Percentage can be explained simply in terms of fractions. Before proceeding further, read the preceding section on fractions as well as the Activity Card Series H.

Per cent comes from the Latin *per centum* meaning "for every hundred". Per cent thus means a ratio or fraction in which the second member is 100. The special symbol for percent—%—is read as "per cent". A per cent can also be written as a ratio or fraction. Thus, 57% can also be written as 57/100. All the rules for working with ratios and fractions also apply to percentage. If you understand fractions, you will easily understand the use of percentages.

The special words sometimes used for percentages are shown in the following formula. percentage = base × rate. In this formula, rate is expressed in hundredths or percent. An example of rate is an *interest rate* of 4%. If a savings bank pays 4% interest and your account contains $100 (the base), the interest you receive ($4) corresponds to the percentage in the above formula. $4 = $100 × 4/100.

If you were given a test with 20 questions and you had 15 correct, what per cent is this? You can express this as the ratio 15/20. From your work with equivalent ratios, you know that you can multiply both the first and the second members of the ratio by any number without changing the value of the ratio. In this case, if you multiply the first and second members of 15/20 by 5, you produce the equivalent ratio (5 × 15)/(5 × 20) = 75/100, which can also be written as .75 or as 75%.

Our system of decimal notation makes it easy to find a per cent by dividing one number by another. (See page 73). Thus, in the example of 15 questions correct on a test of 20 questions, the per cent of correct questions could also have been found by dividing 15 by 20. 15/20 = 15 ÷ 20.

$$
\begin{array}{r}
20 \overline{)\ 15.00} \qquad .7 \\
\underline{14.00} \\
1.00 \qquad .05 \\
\underline{1.00} \\
\hline
.75 = 75\%
\end{array}
$$

V

MATHEMATICAL STRUCTURE

MATHEMATICAL STRUCTURE

The idea of a mathematical structure involves various *members,* and *operations* on these members. The members may be numbers, or they may be sets. The operations performed on the members relate those members of the structure together. For example, the operation of addition relates the numbers 2 and 3 together with 5: 2 + 3 = 5. There are two essential operations in arithmetic, *addition* and *multiplication*. From these are derived the operations of *subtraction* and *division*. In set theory, the operations used are *union* and *intersection*.

The laws or axioms ruling these operations are simple to understand. As they appear continually in today's mathematics, it is important that your child understand these laws, although it is not necessary that he learn the formal language used to express them.

Many different mathematical structures are studied by modern man. Your child, in school and in this Cuisenaire Mathematics Study Kit, will work on developing a mathematical structure called a *field*.

Understanding the rules or laws for working with a field makes it easy for your child to work with numbers. Six laws are listed below and described. They are used elsewhere in this booklet and in the work presented in the Activity Card Series. Do *not* try to work with your child on *all of these laws at once!* Wait until he has some experience with the number relationships of addition and multiplication. (He should understand the content on all Activity Cards through Series J before trying to describe the entire mathematical structure and its laws.)

OUR NUMBER SYSTEM.

Your child will learn in school and in this Cuisenaire Mathematics Study Kit, about *whole numbers, integers, rational numbers,* and *real numbers.*

Whole or natural numbers are those a child uses when he learns to count, plus zero. We can let the set 0, 1, 2, 3, 4, 5, ... etc.

represent the set of *whole* numbers. (The counting numbers, as represented by 1, 2, 3, 4, 5, . . . etc. are a subset of the set of whole numbers.)

Integers are positive and negative numbers and zero. They are easily shown on a number line. Imagine a horizontal line with zero marked at the center. Positive numbers are marked off to the right direction from zero, negative numbers to the left direction from zero. Thus,

$$-5 \quad -4 \quad -3 \quad -2 \quad -1 \quad 0 \quad 1 \quad 2 \quad 3 \quad 4 \quad 5$$

The set of integers can be shown as . . . -5, -4, -3, -2, -1, 0, 1, 2, 3, 4, 5

Rational numbers are numbers that can be written as *ratios* of two integers, the second not being zero. They can be either whole numbers or fractions. A set of rational numbers could be shown as.

. . . $-2/1$, $-3/2$, $-1/1$, $-1/2$, 0, $1/2$, $1/1$, $3/2$, $2/1$ . . . .

$$-2/1 \quad -3/2 \quad -1/1 \quad -1/2 \quad 0 \quad 1/2 \quad 1/1 \quad 3/2 \quad 2/1$$

Real numbers include the rational numbers and the irrational numbers (numbers which cannot be expressed as the ratio of two integers, such as $\sqrt{2}$ or π, the ratio of the circumference of a circle to its diameter). The decimal number system is a representation of the real numbers.

IMBEDDING OF NUMBERS.

Your child will learn about several kinds of numbers. whole numbers, integers (positive and negative numbers and zero) and rational numbers (whole numbers and fractions). It is important that he also learn that *one number can be a whole number, an integer, and a rational number at the same time.* For example. 5 is a whole number. It is also an integer (a positive number) as well as a rational number (5/1).

The various kinds of numbers described so far can be described in set language as follows: {Whole numbers} $\subset$ {Integers (Whole numbers & Negative numbers) } ⊂ {Rational numbers (Integers & Fractions)} ⊂ {Real numbers (Rational numbers & Irrational numbers)}. Just as a small box can be fitted into a larger box, and the latter placed into a still larger box, etc., with the smallest box being at the same time inside all the larger boxes, so can a whole number be imbedded in a sequence of broader concepts of number systems.

FIELD PROPERTIES AND LAWS OF NUMBERS.

In the description of number properties and laws which follow, certain abbreviations will be used.

a, b, and c = any numbers
       W = Whole numbers
        I = Integers (positive and negative whole numbers and zero)
       F = Rational numbers (whole numbers and fractions)
       R = Real numbers

(1)   *Closure Property:*

The numbers (W, I, F, R) are closed under addition. This means that addition of two or more numbers results in a number.

The numbers (W, I, F, R) are closed under multiplication. Multiplication of two numbers results in a number.

(Note: The set of whole numbers and integers (W, I) does not possess the closure property under division. Thus, $10 \div 3 = 3\text{-}1/3$ or $10/3$. This answer is a *rational number* (F) and not the same kind as the original numbers in the problem (W, I). However, the closure property does apply for division of rational numbers. For example. $2/3 \div 1/4 = 8/3$.)

(2)   *Commutative Property:*

The order in which numbers (W, I, F, R) are added does not change the result. Thus, for any numbers a, b.

    a + b = b + a

The order in which numbers (W, I, F, R) are multiplied does not change the result. Thus:

$$a \times b = b \times a$$

(The commutative property does not apply to subtraction and division. Thus, $7 \div 5$ is not the same as $5 \div 7$; or, $6 \div 3$ is not the same as $3 \div 6$.)

(3)　*Associative Property:*

Numbers (W, I, F, R) may be grouped in any combination for addition without changing the value of the sum. Thus, for any numbers a, b, and c:

$$a + b + c = (a + b) + c = a + (b + c)$$

Numbers may be grouped in any combination for multiplication without changing the value of the product. Thus:

$$a \times b \times c = (a \times b) \times c = a \times (b \times c)$$

(4)　*Identity Elements:*

For addition, there is a number, 0, which has the special property that for any number *a* (W, I, F, R):

$$a + 0 = 0 + a = a$$

0 is called the identity element for addition. Add it to a number and the number remains unchanged.

(It will be useful to note here how zero is treated under various circumstances: $a + 0 = a$, $a \times 0 = 0$, $0/a = 0$, $a/0$ has no meaning, $0/0$ has no meaning. Later, when working with exponents (see Glossary), your child will learn that $a^0 = 1$ when $a \neq 0$.)

For multiplication, there is a number, 1, which has the special property that for any number *a* (W, I, F, R):

$$a \times 1 = 1 \times a = a$$

1 is called the identity element for multiplication. Multiply any number by 1 and the number remains unchanged.

Identity elements give meaning to the idea of an *inverse*.

(5) Inverse Elements

For any number a (I, F, R), there is another number a such that a×⁻a = 0. −a is called the *additive inverse* of a. An additive inverse of a number is that number which when added to the original number produces the sum of zero. If a = 5, then ⁻a = ⁻5. If a = ⁻5, then −a = 5. Thus, 5 + (⁻5) = 0. The additive inverse of ⁻5 is 5.

Subtraction is the inverse operation to addition. One undoes the other. Subtraction can be performed by adding the inverse element:

$$5 - 2 = 5 + (- 2)$$

For any number a (F, R) (where a ≠ 0), there is another number a' such that a × a'= 1. a' is called the *multiplication inverse* of a.

(This introduces fractions to our mathematical structure!) If a = 5, then a' = 1/5. If a' = 1/5, then a' = 5.

$$5 \times 1/5 = 1$$

The multiplicative inverse (or *reciprocal*) of a number is that number by which the original number is multiplied to give an answer of 1. Thus:

$$3 \times 1/3 = 1 \quad (1/3) \text{ is the inverse of } 3)$$
$$5/4 \times 4/5 = 20/20 = 1 \quad (4/5 \text{ is the inverse of } 5/4)$$

Division can thus be seen as an inverse operation to multiplication. Thus:

$$10 \div 2 = 10 \times 1/2 = 10/2 = 5$$

(6) Distributive Property:

The separate operations of addition and multiplication (W, I, F, R) are related by this property. Thus, for any numbers a, b, and c:

$$a + (b \times c) \neq (a + b) \times (a + c)$$

If a, b, and c are real numbers, then a × (b + c) = ab + ac. With this property, *multiplication is distributed over addition.* The reverse is *not* true: in general, addition cannot be distributed over multiplication:

$$a + (b \times c) \neq (a + b) \times (a + c)$$

It may be interesting to note here that while in arithmetic there is only one distributive property, namely—multiplication over addition, in set theory there are two. union over intersection, and intersection over union. Thus:

$$A \cup (B \cap C) = (A \cup B) \cap (A \cup C) \text{ and}$$
$$A \cap (B \cup C) = (A \cap B) \cup (A \cap C)$$

We include this observation to demonstrate that the structure of arithmetic is not the only possible structure for a mathematical system.

The above six laws are used in your child's school mathematics and in this Cuisenaire Mathematics Study Kit as the basic foundation for the study of all the arithmetic and algebra he will study until he meets *complex numbers* (see Glossary).

BIBLIOGRAPHY

You and your child may wish to explore mathematics further. The following selected materials are available from the Cuisenaire Company of America, Inc.

Mathematics Illustrated Dictionary — Bendick and Levin. (McGraw-Hill)
Move In On Math — Whittaker (Cuisenaire)
Cosmic View: The Universe in 40 Jumps — Boeke (Day)
You and Me — Kimball (Activity Resources)
Altair Design — Holiday (Pantheon)
The I Hate Mathematics Book — Burns (Little, Brown)
Measuring In Metric — Siderman (Cuisenaire)
2, 4, 6, 8, Let's Start to Calculate — Davidson (Cuisenaire)
Boggle — Vine (Price/Stern/Sloan)
Calculator Puzzles, Tricks and Games — Pallas (Sterling)
Calculator Explorations — Miller (Cuisenaire)
Geoboard Activity Kit (Learning Games)
Triman Compass (Cuisenaire)
Domodots (Cuisenaire)

VI

MATHEMATICS GLOSSARY AND INDEX

This section combines a mathematics glossary with an index to both this book and the accompanying Activity Cards. Where there is a reference to the book or the cards, you will find the topic is treated in more detail and in context. Page numbers refer to pages in this book, and the Activity Cards are referred to by a letter for the series and a numeral for the particular card in the series. When a word in a definition is in bold face, you may find it helpful to look up that word also in this glossary.

Addition, 33, 64, A-5, G-2

One of the fundamental operations of arithmetic. It associates with two numbers, called *addends,* a third number, their *sum.* Thus, in 2 + 3 = 5, two and three are the addends, and five is the sum.

Additive Inverse—see **Inverse Element**

Associative Property (or Law), 34, 36, 84

1. For **addition,** the sum of three numbers is not dependent on the order in which they are grouped. Thus, 2 + (3 + 5) = (2 + 3) + 5 = 10

2. For **multiplication,** the product of three numbers is not dependent on the order in which they are grouped. Thus, 2 × (3 × 5) = (2 × 3) × 5 = 30

3. An **operation** is associative if, for any three elements being combined under the operation, the result does not depend on how the elements are grouped (without changing the order). This property holds for the arithmetic operations of addition and multiplication and for the set operations of union and intersection.

Axiom (or postulate)

A fundamental proposition in mathematics which is assumed rather than proved. In this Kit, the Fundamental Laws on pages 81-86 are examples of axioms.

Base

1. The base in a numeration system is the number whose powers are used to construct the system. Our usual notation

uses ten as the base of the *decimal system,* and the other systems used are called non-decimal bases. See Card I-4 & pages 30-31.

2. In geometry, the side or face on which a figure is presumed to stand.

3. The base of a system of logarithms is that number for which the exponents of its powers are the logarithms of the system.

4. In **percentage:** the number of which some percentage is to be found.

Binary—see **Operation** and **Numeration**

Cardinal number—see **Number,** 47, A-6

Cartesian product

The Cartesian product of two sets A and B is the set of all **ordered pairs** (*a, b*) such that *a* belongs to A and *b* to B. It is shown as A × B.

Clock arithmetic—see **Modular arithmetic**

Closure, 33, 35, 83

A system of numbers is closed under an operation if the result of the operation upon two members of the system is always another member of the system. Thus, the whole numbers are closed under multiplication and addition.

Coefficient, 31, I-3

The numerical factor of a term in algebra; a number written before a quantity to indicate how many times the quantity is to be taken. Thus, in the term $2x^3$, 2 is the coefficient.

Commutative Property (or LAW), 33, 36, 83

1. An **operation** is commutative if, for any elements being combined under the operation, changing the order of the elements does not change the result. This property applies to the arithmetic operations of addition and multiplication and the set operations of union and intersection.

2. For **addition,** the sum of two numbers is not dependent on the order in which they are added. Thus, $2 + 3 = 3 + 2 = 5$.

3. For **multiplication,** the product of two numbers does not depend on the order in which they are multiplied. Thus, 2 × 3 = 3 × 2 = 6.

Complement, 48, E-3A, G-2

1. See **set**

2. The difference between a given angle and 90°

3. The difference between a number and a given number; in particular, the difference between a number and a unit of the next higher order: thus, 4 is the complement of 6 (in the unit of 10) and 24 is the complement of 76 (in the unit of 100).

Congruent

1. Two numbers are congruent when they have the same remainder after being divided by a third number *(the modulus).* Thus, 9 and 16 are congruent, modulus 7, since the remainder for both 9 and 16 is 2 after dividing by 7.

2. In plane geometry, two figures are congruent if one can be fitted exactly over the other.

Correspondence (same as mapping), A-4

1. A matching of members of one set with members of another set (or the same set).

2. One-to-one correspondence is an exact matching of members from one set with members from another set, so that the members match exactly. An example is the matching of one's fingers with one's toes.

3. Many-valued correspondence is a matching of a member from one set with more than one member from another set. An example is matching people with their parents, so that each person is matched with his two parents.

Cuisenaire, Georges, 17-18

Decimal — see **Numeration** and **Fraction**

Denominator — see **Fraction**

Digit — see **Numeral**

Distributive Law, 37-40, 85-86, G-4

1. Multiplication is tied to addition by the distributive property (or Law). For any three numbers, a, b and c, it states that $a \times (b + c) = (a \times b) + (a \times c)$.

2. Union distributes over intersection: A ∪ (B ∩ C) = (A ∪ B) ∩ (A ∪ C).

3. Intersection distributes over union:
A ∩ (B ∪ C = (A ∩ B) ∪ (A ∩ C)

Division, 36-37, 71-74, G-5

Division is the inverse operation to multiplication. Thus, if $7 \times 9 = 63$, then $63 \div 7 = 9$. In $a \div b = c$ (or $a/b = c$), a is the *dividend*, b is the *divisor* and c is the *quotient*.

Element—see **Set**

Empty Set — see **Set**

Equal Sets, 47, C-4

Sets are equal which contain exactly the same members. These are also called identical sets.

Equality — see **Equivalence Relation**

Equation, 42-44, B-1

A *mathematical sentence* stating the equality of two quantities. Thus, $A = B$ or $5 + 4 = 3 \times 3$

Equivalence Relation

1. An equivalence relation is a rule for associating two elements, which satisfies each of the following conditions:

(a) (Reflexive) The relation associates each element with itself.
(b) (Symmetric) If a is related to b, then b is related to a.
(c) (Transitive) If a is related to b, and b is related to c, then a is related to c.

2. Examples of equivalence relations are:

"has the same parents", "is in the same homeroom". Equality is an equivalence relation.

3. Equivalence between sets means that the members of one set can be matched exactly or put into one-to-one correspondence. An example is the set of your fingers and the set of your toes. Since these two sets can be matched exactly, they are equivalent.

Equivalent Expression, G-1

Equivalent Sets — see **Set**, 47, C-4

Exponent — see **Power**, I-2

Factor, 68

A number *a* is a factor of a second number *b* if *a* divides evenly into *b;* that is $b = a \times c$ with *a, b,* and *c* all whole numbers. Thus, 5 is a factor of 15 since $15 = 5 \times 3$.

A *prime factor* is a factor which is a **prime number**.

The *highest common factor* of two numbers is the largest number which is a factor of both numbers.

Field Properties, 83-86

Figure
1. See **Numeral**
2. In geometry — a drawing

Finite Arithmetic — see **Modular Arithmetic**

Fraction, 74-77, D-3-5, H-1-5

The ratio of two integers, a/b, with *b* not equal to zero. An example is 3/5 or 5/2.

The ratio of 5/2 may be written as $\frac{5}{2}$ or as (5, 2).

The first member of the ratio is called the *numerator* and the second member is called the *denominator*.

A *unit fraction* is a fraction whose numerator is one.

A *decimal fraction* such as .345 can always be expressed as a ratio, the example also being written as 345/1000.

Function

A subset of the **Cartesian product** of two sets in which no two different ordered pairs have the same first member. An example is a set of ordered pairs in which the first members are married men and the second members are the corresponding wives. Another example is the set of ordered pairs (x, y) such that $x^2 = y$.

Greater Than — see **Inequalities**

Identity Element (neutral element), 34, 36, 84

1. An identity (or neutral) element is an element which, when combined with any other element under a given operation, leaves that other element unchanged.

2. For **addition**, the identity element is 0. Its special property is that adding it to any number does not change that number.

3. For **multiplication,** the identity element is 1. Its special property is that multiplying any number by it does not change that number.

4. For set union, the identity element is the empty set.

Inclusion — see **Set,** C-2B

Inequity, B-2B

1. A statement that the equality relation does not hold. The notation for this is $\neq$.

2. In arithmetic, if $a \neq b$, then a must be either greater than b $(a > b)$ or less than b $(a < b)$.

Intersection, see **Set,** 48, 49, C-4

Inverse Element, 85

1. For **addition,** the *additive inverse* of a number is that number which, when added to it, has zero for a sum. Thus, the additive inverse of 3 is -3, since $3 + (-3) = 0$. The additive inverse of -3 is $-(-3) = +3$

2. For **multiplication,** the *multiplicative inverse* of a number is that number which, when multiplied by the first number, produces 1 (the **identity element** for multiplication) as the

product. Thus, the multiplicative inverse of 5 is $1/5$ since $5 \times 1/5 = 1$. The multiplicative inverse is also called the *reciprocal* of a number.

3. The inverse of an element under a given operation is that element which, when combined with the original element, produces the identity element for that operation.

Inverse Operation

An inverse operation is an operation which undoes the operation of which it is the inverse. Thus, subtraction is the inverse operation to addition, and subtracting 5 undoes the effect of adding 5. Dividing by 7 undoes the effect of multiplying by 7. Not all operations have inverses.

Least Common Multiple

The least common multiple of two or more numbers is the smallest number which each of these numbers will divide evenly without a remainder. For example, 12 is the lowest common multiple of 2, 3, 4, and 6.

Less Than — see Inequalities

Mapping — same as Correspondence

Matching — see Correspondence

Mathematical Sentence, 32

1. A *closed sentence* is a statement which can be shown to be true or false. Example: $2 \times 3 = 8$ (false)

2. An *open sentence* is a statement containing a variable, such as $2 + \square = 9$. Its truth or falsity cannot be determined until the variable is assigned a value.

Measure, D-2, D-5

Comparison to some unit which is agreed upon as a standard. Examples are inches, metres, pounds, hours.

Member — see Set

Metric System — K-1-3

The decimal system of measure based on the metre and the gram as the standard units. It is the standard system for everyday measure for most countries, and the standard used for work in science in the United States as well as the rest of the world. The Cuisenaire colored rods are built around this standard, with the white rod being one cubic centimetre. The metric system is a legal system of measure now being adopted officially throughout the United States.

Minus Sign (–)

1. It is the sign used to indicate the operation of subtraction. It is read as 'minus'.

2. It is used as the sign for the negative of a number. Thus, the negative of 4 is –4. The negative of –4 is 4.

Mixed Number

The sum of a whole number and a fraction, such as 7-3/5. This is the same number as 38/5, and either is an acceptable form of notation.

Modular Arithmetic, 50-52

(also called *clock arithmetic* or *finite arithmetic*)

An arithmetic using only a stated number of elements. One example is the days of the week, which is a finite set having only seven members which are then repeated. Another example is our clock, which has only twelve numbers on it. In this system, if we add 5 to 10 the result is 3, not 15, since 5 hours later than 10 o'clock is 3 o'clock.

Multiple, F-4

A number which is the *product* of two other numbers, called *factors.*

Multiplication, 35-37, 67-71, F-4, G-4, H-4

One of the fundamental operations of arithmetic. It associates with two numbers, called *factors,* a third number called their *product.* Thus, in $3 \times 4 = 12$, 3 and 4 are the factors, and 12 is the product.

Negative Number, J-1-2

Negative Of A Number — same as **Additive Inverse**

Null Set — see **Set**

Number, 29, 81-86, A-6, J-1

Number is an abstract concept that should not be confused with the names and symbols we call numerals.

Positive numbers are numbers greater than zero.

Negative numbers are numbers less than zero.

Counting numbers are the numbers 1, 2, 3, 4, . . . They are usually defined as being properties of sets. Thus, all sets that can be matched exactly share the same cardinal number, and have the same counting number attached to them.

Whole numbers are counting numbers with the addition of zero (also called cardinal numbers).

Integers are the whole numbers and their additive **inverses.** They include numbers such as 5, – 5.

Rational numbers are those numbers which can be constructed from the whole numbers through the operations of addition, subtraction, multiplication, and division. The rational numbers include such numbers as 5, - 5, 1/5, 3/5, and - 3/5. Every whole number, integer, and fraction is at the same time a rational number.

Prime numbers are whole numbers which have no factors other than one and the number itself.

Composite numbers are all whole numbers which are not prime.

Real numbers. We also use numbers which are not rational numbers, including such numbers as $\sqrt{2}$ and π (ratio of circumference of a circle to its diameter). The set of real numbers includes all such numbers as well as the rational numbers.

The *cardinal number* of a set is a number which describes the number of elements in the set.

Ordinal numbers are numbers that specify the order or position of a member or element of a set. Thus, first, second, third, etc.

Number Line

A line on which points are associated with numbers in a one-to-one correspondence; the line represents a set of numbers. A number line is often used as a model for work with numbers.

$$\overset{\displaystyle \xleftarrow{\hspace{3em}} \quad \underset{-5}{\text{|}} \quad \underset{-4}{\text{|}} \quad \underset{-3}{\text{|}} \quad \underset{-2}{\text{|}} \quad \underset{-1}{\text{|}} \quad \underset{0}{\text{|}} \quad \underset{1}{\text{|}} \quad \underset{2}{\text{|}} \quad \underset{3}{\text{|}} \quad \underset{4}{\text{|}} \quad \underset{5}{\text{|}} \quad \xrightarrow{\hspace{3em}}}{}$$

Numeral (or figure), 29, B-4

The name or symbols, either spoken or written, for a number. Here are some examples of numerals: two, 7, 235, XIV. A *digit* is one of the symbols 0, 1, 2, 3, 4, 5, 6, 7, 8, 9

Numeration, 30-31, I-1-5

A system of sequentially naming and writing the names of numbers. It is usually applied to place value systems, such as our *usual decimal system* of numeration. Such a system is based on powers of a number, in this case ten. Other systems are possible and are used in practice and taught in schools. These other systems are called non-decimal, and include the *binary* (based on powers of 2), *octal* (based on 8), *and duodecimal* (based on 12). See **base.**

Numerator — see **Fraction**

Open Sentence — see **Mathematical Sentence**

Operation

1. An operation is a rule for combining members of a set to form another member of the set.
2. The fundamental **operations** of arithmetic are addition and multiplication. Their **inverse operations** are subtraction and division.
3. The fundamental operations of set theory are union and intersection.

Order of Operations, 40

Ordered Pair, 49-50

A set containing two elements in which the order of the listing is significant. An ordered pair is listed within parentheses rather than braces.

Thus, the ordered pair (5, 2) is not the same as the ordered pair (2, 5).

The idea of ordered pairs can be generalized to ordered triples and quadruples. For example, the ordered triple (38, 24, 38) is not the same as (24, 38, 38).

Ordinal Number — see **Number,** A-6

Parentheses, E-3B, 40

Percentage, 77-78

A special notation for **fractions** or ratios whose second member is 100. Thus, 57% = 57/100.

Placeholder — see **Variable**

Place Value — see **Numeration,** 30-31, 66-67, F-1, I-1

Polynomial

1. An expression such as $ax^3 + bx^2 + cx + d$.
2. The expanded form of a number name, such as 435 when written out as $4 \times 10^2 + 3 \times 10 + 5$, is the polynomial form of the numeral.

Positive Number — see **Number,** J-1

Power, I-2

The power of a number is the result obtained by taking that number as a **factor** as many times as specified by a number called the *exponent.*

An example is 2^3, in which the '3' represents the exponent. This is read as 'two to the third power' and has the same meaning as $2 \times 2 \times 2 = 8$. Any number to the first power is that number itself, and any number (except 0) to the zero power is defined as equal to one.

A negative exponent indicates the reciprocal of the power indicated.

The **inverse operation** of raising to a power is taking the *root* of a number and is indicated by a unit fractional exponent. Thus, $8^{1/3}$ is the undoing of 2^3 (this may also be shown as $\sqrt[3]{8}$).

Product — see **Multiplication**

Pronumeral — see **Variable**

Proportion
An equality of two ratios: $a/b = c/d$

Quotient— see **Division**

Ratio, H-1

Rational Number — see **Number**

Reciprocal — see **Inverse Element, H-1**

Reflexive — see **Equivalence Relation**

Relation
A relation is a set of **ordered pairs**. A member, b, is related to a member a in a particular relation if the ordered pair (a, b) is an element of this set of ordered pairs. An example is the set of ordered pairs representing married couples. A given pair belongs to the set if the second person named is the wife of the first person named. Also see **equivalence relation.**

Root — see **Power**

Scientific Notation
Scientific notation is a way of expressing numbers as a product of a number between 1 and 10 and a power of 10.
An example is 3.52×10^3. This is particularly useful in expressing very large and very small numbers. $3.52 \times 10^3 = 3,520$, while $3.52 \times 10^{-3} = .00352$.

Sequence, A-3B

A succession of numbers (or other elements) placed in order in correspondence with the counting numbers. 1, 2, 3, 4, 5, ... is an example of a sequence. 2, 4, 6, 8, 10, ... is another example of a sequence. If it is an unending sequence in which there is never a last term it is called an *infinite sequence*. If there is a last term in the sequence it is called a *finite sequence*.

Series

The sum of the terms of a **sequence**. Thus, the sum of the sequence 1, 2, 4, 8, 16 is 1 + 2 + 4 + 8 + 16 = 31. If the sequence is finite it is called a finite series, and if the sequence is infinite it is called an infinite series. An example of an infinite series is the sum of the sequence 1, 2, 3, 4, 5, 6, 7, 8, ...

Set, 46-50, C-1-4

A collection of objects. This is a fundamental idea in mathematics. Every adult should refer to pages 46-50 to make sure he/she understands this!

A set contains *members* or *elements* which belong to the set. The *empty set* (void or null set) is the set with no members. Example. set of female U.S. presidents.

A subset of a set is a set of which every member is also a member of the set *containing* the subset.

Equal sets are sets which contain exactly the same members.

Equivalent sets are sets whose members can be matched exactly (put into one-to-one correspondence).

The *cardinal number* of a set is the number of distinct members contained in the set. The cardinal number of the empty set is zero. (The idea of cardinality is further extended in advanced mathematics.)

The *intersection* of two sets is the set which contains each member that is a member of both sets.

The *union* of two sets is the set which contains each member that belongs to either set, with no member counted twice.

Disjoint sets are sets which have no member in common.

Signed Number, J-1-3

Solution Set

The set of replacements for the **variable** in an open **mathematical sentence** which makes the sentence into a true statement.

Subset — see **Set**

Subtraction, 33-35, 37, 65-67, 85 A-5A, G-3

Subtraction is the inverse operation to addition. Thus, if $3 + 2 = 5$, then $5 - 3 = 2$. In $a - b = c$, a is the *minuend*, b the *subtrahend* and *c* is the *difference* (or remainder).

Sum — see **Addition**

Symmetric — see **Equivalence Relation**

Symmetry, A-5B

Transitive — see **Equivalence Relation**

Truth Set — see **Solution Set**

Union — see **Set**

Unknown

1. See **Variable**

2. Sometimes used to describe the missing element in word problems

Variable (also called unknown, placeholder, frame, pronumeral, 'box')

A symbol used to stand for a number or quantity in a **mathematical sentence.** In the following examples, the symbols $\square$, x, y, ? are all used as variables: $3 + \square = 8$; $x^2 = 9$; $y > 4$; $5 - ? = 2$.

The set of numerals which may be used to replace the variable in a mathematical sentence is known as a *replacement set.*

The subset of the replacement set which makes the mathematical sentence into a true statement is called the *solution set.*

Venn Diagrams, 48

Venn diagrams are diagrams which illustrate set operations such as union, intersection, and complement.

Word Problems, 44-45

HOW TO GET MORE INFORMATION ON
MATHEMATICS LEARNING PRODUCTS

We have attempted in this Kit to answer the questions your children and you are most likely to ask about mathematics learning. We will be very glad to learn how useful the Kit is or has been to your children and you, and to incorporate your suggestions into later editions. If you have additional questions about any topic covered which you believe should have been answered in this Kit, or wish to receive information on other mathematical learning products, please write to.

CUISENAIRE COMPANY OF AMERICA, INC.
12 Church Street
New Rochelle, N.Y. 10801